THE
PAST LIFE
PERSPECTIVE

To Jeanette

Enjoy exploring —

Many happy "returns"

[signature]

THE
PAST LIFE
PERSPECTIVE

Discovering Your True Nature
Across Multiple Lifetimes

ANN C. BARHAM, MA, LMFT

ATRIA
—
ENLIVEN BOOKS

New York   London   Toronto   Sydney   New Delhi

ATRIA BOOKS

ENLIVEN

An Imprint of Simon & Schuster, Inc.
1230 Avenue of the Americas
New York, NY 10020

First Enliven trade paperback edition June 2016

This publication contains the opinions and ideas of its author. It is intended to provide helpful and informative material on the subjects addressed in the publication. It is sold with the understanding that the author and publisher are not engaged in rendering medical, health, or any other kind of personal professional services in the book. The reader should consult his or her medical, health, or other competent professional before adopting any of the suggestions in this book or drawing inferences from it.

The author and publisher specifically disclaim all responsibility for any liability, loss, or risk, personal or otherwise, which is incurred as a consequence, directly or indirectly, of the use and application of any of the contents of this book.

For information about special discounts for bulk purchases, please contact Simon & Schuster Special Sales at 1-866-506-1949 or business@simonandschuster.com.

The Simon & Schuster Speakers Bureau can bring authors to your live event. For more information or to book an event, contact the Simon & Schuster Speakers Bureau at 1-866-248-3049 or visit our website at www.simonspeakers.com.

Interior design by Kyoko Watanabe

Library of Congress Cataloging-in-Publication Data is available.

Manufactured in the United States of America

10 9 8 7 6 5 4 3 2 1

ISBN 978-1-5011-3573-6
ISBN 978-1-5011-3574-3 (ebook)

Dedicated with love to three very special people who have made their transitions to their next adventures:

Dr. Ron Scolastico, spiritual teacher and gifted channeler. Thank you for your wisdom, which has led to a deeper understanding of the eternal realities. Your twinkling eyes and profound guidance are sorely missed.

Margaret "Meg" Keller, licensed marriage and family therapist, counselor extraordinaire, valued colleague, beloved friend, and co-adventurer in spirit.

And last but certainly not least, my dear mother, Antoinette "Toni" Gattuccio Conrad, who did her best to wrap her mind around the unusual thing her daughter did for a living. I'm sure it's all perfectly clear to you now!

The nature of our immortal lives is in the consequences of our words and deeds, that go on and are pushing themselves throughout all time . . . From womb to tomb, we are bound to others, past and present, and by each crime and every kindness, we birth our future.

—DAVID MITCHELL, *CLOUD ATLAS*,
"THE REVELATION OF SONMI 451"

Souls cross ages like clouds cross skies, an' tho' a cloud's shape nor hue nor size don't stay the same, it's still a cloud an' so is a soul. Who can say where the cloud's blowed from or who the soul'll be 'morrow?

—DAVID MITCHELL, *CLOUD ATLAS*,
"ZACHRY"

Contents

THE

PAST LIFE
PERSPECTIVE

INTRODUCTION

"I WONDER IF I've had a past life?" or "Can past life therapy really help me?" In my last seventeen years as a marriage and family therapist specializing in past life regression, I've had my share of clients who express some healthy skepticism. It's hard for many people to initially fathom the possibility that they may have experienced a prior life even once, let alone many dozens of times. Like the proverbial cat with nine lives, we've faced death many, many times, only to see our spirits live again in another lifetime. Indications are, we've more than equaled those clever felines, and we're still counting! It's just that in each lifetime we show up in a different body and personality, and most of us don't remember what's come before without some assistance. That's where past life therapy comes in.

You are about to read a selection of fascinating and insightful case studies taken from my files working with past life regression clients. ("Regression" simply means going back, so past life regression is literally going back to past lifetimes.) Although certain case studies jumped out immediately as must-share stories, you have no idea how difficult it was to decide which ones to include and which to save for another day. You will see an amazing variety in the type of clients who have consulted me and the past life stories that were revealed in session. All of these clients were happy to give me a release to share their regressions with you; in fact, it is extremely rare for a client to be unwilling to share his/her story. Of course, names have been changed and identifying information protected so that client confidentiality is maintained.

Many readers might ask: "Are these stories real?" The information in each of these case studies was directly told by the client while in a live session and was transcribed from copious notes and audio files I keep. A past life therapy session is quite different from a psychic reading, in which information is provided to the client through an intermediary. With past life regression, all the information is coming directly from the client by accessing unconscious memories via hypnosis or a similar technique. In these case studies, I include quotes straight from my clients where appropriate, including their occasional grammatical inconsistencies and unique ways of saying things. I want to give a clear and authentic picture of what it's like to go through a regression.

As far as the legitimacy of these client stories as true past life experiences, one of the great things about being a past life therapist as opposed to a researcher is that I have nothing to prove regarding the validity of the information that clients bring up in session. Rather than *Is this really true or not?* the questions I ask myself as a therapist are: *Does this help people? Are they able to understand themselves better? Deal with challenges more effectively? Unlock dysfunctional dynamics in relationships they've been struggling with? Identify more closely with the eternal nature of their existence?* In short, does integrating knowledge from their prior lifetimes help them move more fully into realizing their potential in their current lives? Since in most cases the answer to the above questions has been a resounding yes, then it doesn't really matter from a therapeutic perspective if their past life memories are 100 percent correct or not.

Of course we all know that even our memories in our current lives are far from perfectly accurate. The classic story we've all heard is of the policeman who interviews three different witnesses of a traffic accident and gets three different versions of what happened. So inaccuracies are just part of the territory when anyone is dealing with perception and memory. When I approach the past life memories of a client, I'm looking for the emotional impact of the event: What meaning did that past life personality attach to it? What thoughts or decisions arose as a result? How are these events, thoughts, and decisions impacting the client now in his/her current life? What insights can we integrate so the client can move forward more freely?

———

Occasionally, clients worry after the regression that maybe they "just made it up" or it was only their imagination. In the scheme of things, that isn't particularly important. In the first place, we can treat the past life stories as illustrative metaphors for the issues and influences in a person's current life. It gives us very rich material to work with, as any therapist who employs dream interpretation, creative imagery, sand tray work, or other projective techniques well knows. And as far as imagination goes, where does imagination come from, anyway? For all we know, much of what we label imagination or daydreaming may well be past life material creeping in. It just hasn't been identified as such.

And if the story we're working with is made up, why was it that particular story? Why is it often a story so unexpected by the clients, something they maintain they would never imagine in their wildest dreams? Places in the world they have never been, time periods they know very little about, personalities that seem odd or foreign—all of these factors arise. In all but a few cases the lifetimes uncovered are not illustrious and may in fact be filled with the daily events of rather mundane lives. At times I've even had clients burst out with "What a boring lifetime that was!" (And, frankly, I had to agree with them.) It's extremely rare to have a king, queen, or famous personality emerge. If the client is making the story up, wouldn't we expect to have more stories that were predictable or impressive?

In my work, I have come to believe that most of the prior lifetimes that clients have recalled are indeed "real," even if all the details aren't accurate or filled in. Perhaps what convinces me more than anything else is that I have witnessed such depths of emotion from many clients as they relive the events of a prior lifetime. Anyone might shed a few tears while watching a touching movie or reading a great novel, but to sob in anguish at the death of a loved one in a prior life is a little far-fetched if the client just made this up from his/her imagination. However, I have also learned over the years that an obvious cathartic release is not a necessary ingredient for a successful regression. More than once I have gone through a session with a client who shows little emotion in the exploration of the memories, only to comment at the end of the session, "Oh my gosh, that was so intense!" We each experience dramatic events in our own way.

Dramatic or not, releasing the grief and emotion does seem to have a lasting effect on clients. Touching the reality of their spiritual nature also seems to stay with them. One particular area involves death. I have many clients tell me that after a regression they have lost their fear of death. The experience of going through the death of a prior personality, realizing that their consciousness continues and almost universally goes to a place of deep peace and unity, and seeing the past life connections with loved ones from the current lifetime—all of these personal insights alter one's understanding of that mysterious transition.

In addition to offering tremendous benefits to individuals working to live fuller lives, I believe past life regression can also do a great service to humanity in general. With all the negativity and worries we hear about and face today, it's easy to wonder where we have gone wrong as a species. I recall a morning not long ago when a radio talk show host was discussing some recent incidences of senseless violence: a young collegiate ballplayer was run down and shot in the back by three young men ages fifteen, sixteen, and seventeen. They killed him for no other reason than that they were "feeling bored." A few days later, an eighty-eight-year-old war veteran was assaulted by two sixteen-year-old youths as he was entering his local club. They beat him brutally with flashlights, and he died the next day of his injuries. Again, his attackers did this for no apparent reason. And this is to say nothing of the terrorist attacks that have become more and more frequent.

Events like these evoke such a deep sense of dismay and sadness in me, and I wonder: How can there be so little empathy and kindness for our fellow human beings? How have we become so divided between "them" and "us" that some of our youth do not feel a common bond of humanity between themselves and those they attack?

The understanding came to me that past life therapy is one of the best ways to reestablish that sense of human commonality. When we delve into our prior lifetimes, we face the great equalizer. We see that we have been both male and female; Christian and Jew and Muslim and pagan; wealthy and privileged as well as a beggar on the streets; violent offender as well as victim. Across the many centuries of our experience, each of us has probably been on both sides of every fence. "They," indeed, are truly "us."

Can we learn to treat each other with kindness, compassion, and love despite the outward differences that we may exhibit in our current lives and personalities? It is my hope that by sharing some of the case studies in this book, readers can learn more about what past life therapy is and how it might benefit them in their own lives. The studies will serve as a reminder to avoid the quick rush to judgment toward others: we've been there; we've done that too. Or if we haven't yet, we may very well in future lifetimes. Hopefully, the lesson of the oneness of humanity will truly be learned in the not-too-distant future. I think the growing acceptance and credibility of prior lifetimes, and the increasing number of people who have experienced their own past lives, will have a role in this collective transition.

My mission in writing *The Past Life Perspective*, therefore, is to help advance your understanding and demystify past life therapy as well as demonstrate how recalling and integrating the knowledge of our own prior lifetimes can heal and propel each of us forward in our own personal development. By sharing these fascinating client studies, I also hope to contribute to the evolving consciousness that there is no true foundation for the divisiveness between people on the planet, in short, to expand our perspective on the human condition. I welcome you to my world as a past life therapist.

CHAPTER 1

Out of the New Age and into the Mainstream

MY COUNSELING career started out fairly conventionally. I earned my master's degree in counseling psychology from Santa Clara University—a Jesuit university, no less—in the world-famous Silicon Valley of California. And I became licensed as a marriage and family therapist by the state of California in due course. In the midst of my studies, I took a course entitled Therapeutic Imagery. My professor, the late Dr. William Yabroff, was highly regarded but seen as just slightly eccentric within the very conventional Santa Clara faculty; his specialty was the use of guided imagery to deal with psychological and physical symptoms. To my surprise and curiosity, toward the end of the course he introduced the idea that at times clients experience imagery that could be interpreted as past life memory. He claimed he wanted us to be familiar with what this might look like, just in case we encountered it. I learned later that he was very much involved with the regression community at large; this was his way of quietly introducing his passion into the straitlaced Santa Clara program.

My professor described the issues that might be related to a past lifetime—some recurring physical ailment, an unresolved relationship dynamic—and asked for volunteers, as he was going to demonstrate a past life regression right there in class. I immediately raised my hand.

I recently had undergone surgery on both of my pinky toes due to a condition known as rotated hammer toe, which means the toe lies a bit on its side and slips partway under the neighboring toe, causing the joint to point sideways and rub painfully against the sides of one's shoes. This had given me some trouble for a few years, but despite surgery and ultrasound treatments afterwards, I was still experiencing pain that interfered with many of my favorite athletic activities.

I lay down on the carpet in the front of a class of about a dozen people. My professor used a gentle hypnotic induction to put me in a relaxed state, then directed me to the time and place where the problem with my feet originated. I was startled to find myself seeing/sensing an adolescent girl with Asian features and identifying with her. Then the story just began to roll out from there: she/I was extremely upset because my family had insisted on binding my feet. Not only was it painful, it limited my ability to move about and do things!

Unusual for that culture and time period, I was a rather strong-willed young girl, and I decided to defy authority and tradition. With the help of a household servant, I made a plan to run away, but I was caught in the act. This defiant action was considered a terrible disgrace for my family and particularly for my father, who had some position of note in the community. He eventually disowned me and sold me into servitude. I saw images of me walking barefoot and in rags over rough and rocky terrain to a place far from my home. I knew that I was in eternal shame for dishonoring my father. I worked for some time as a kitchen servant, and eventually I used one of the kitchen knives to take my own life because I could no longer bear the disgrace of my position.

Dr. Yabroff moved me through the death experience and into a brief life review, looking at the key lessons, decisions, and attitudes carried forward from that lifetime. Some of these focused on the conflict between loyalty to the family versus following my own path—playing it safe versus rocking the boat. Challenging paternal authority seemed to be a pattern that I had carried forward and continued in my current life, along with the belief that I really had to fight for what I believed. The most amazing part of the experience, however, was the fact that my legs quivered uncontrollably as I lay in front of the classroom. It wasn't painful, however. It was as if my legs were releasing some sort of energy that had been stored in them since that prior lifetime. (I can't totally explain how this works, but I've also had clients shake during sessions as energy is being released. It seems that the physical body can hold on to trauma in some representative manner, a little like birthmarks that we sometimes see that are related to injuries in prior lifetimes.) To my astonishment and that of my classmates, I was back on the tennis court the following day with no foot distress, and those toes have never bothered me again in the twenty-plus years since then.

I am in no way claiming that past life work will cure a myriad of physical complaints in one fell swoop, but from this personal experience and from my own private practice, I have seen that it can sometimes make a real difference when modern medicine has hit a block. And as you can imagine, after this first experience with regression in front of the class, my interest to learn more about past life therapy was sparked.

The next occasion I had to delve deeper into this unconventional therapeutic approach came after I had started my private practice. Two of the world's renowned past life experts of the time, Dr. Brian Weiss and the late British Jungian therapist Dr. Roger Woolger, came for weeklong training workshops at a retreat center near my home. Each workshop was uniquely different from the other, and each was a truly marvelous experience. As participants in the workshops, we watched demonstrations given by true masters in the art of past life regression, each with his own distinctive style.

I was fortunate enough to have Dr. Woolger work directly with me on a theme I described as "being intolerant of ignorant men," which the rest of the training group voted as the issue they found most enticing. Dr. Woolger regressed me first to a lifetime as a natural healer in the early American colonies, accused of witchcraft by the doctors and community leaders ("those ignorant men"). I was eventually shipped back to France, where I'd come from. The issue linked back further to a lifetime as a Viking raider who died from an axe through the skull in a skirmish over a woman. (I had been quite a thickheaded and ignorant man myself, it appears!)

Of course, as workshop participants, we also had many opportunities to practice leading regressions on each other. Afterwards, I began to experiment with friends and open-minded clients in my practice, continuing to gather techniques and knowledge from other past life therapists as I went along, eventually building my own distinct style. A hallmark of my approach to past life work is the amount of time I spend processing prior life experience and lessons with the client so that he/she can integrate these realizations into daily life. I found the work exciting and rewarding, and the lack of dependence that traditional clients sometimes develop in conventional therapy was quite refreshing to me. Gradually my practice has evolved to the point where I focus almost entirely on past life work.

Demystifying Past Life Therapy

Although the public perception of reincarnation or past lives used to evoke jokes about Shirley MacLaine "hanging" *Out on a Limb* (well, at least for those of us over a certain age), millions have read books on the subject. Its public image doesn't accurately reflect what people believe in private: a Gallup Poll taken in 2001 showed that 25 percent of adult Americans admitted anonymously that they believed in reincarnation.[1] An online Harris Poll in November 2013 similarly put the overall number of believers at 24 percent, an increase from 20 percent in 2009.[2] In both polls, an additional 27 percent of Americans admitted that they didn't disbelieve in reincarnation; they just didn't know. And a 2010 article in the *New York Times* written by Lisa Miller, a religion editor for *Newsweek* magazine, explored the growing Western belief in reincarnation. The article quoted a Spanish bishop who indicated that a growing number of Catholics (28 percent) had adopted a belief in reincarnation.[3]

In the general public, there are a growing number of popular films and books about reincarnation that have gained much recognition. The Thai film *Uncle Boonmee Who Can Recall His Past Lives* was awarded the Palme d'Or, the highest prize at the Cannes Film Festival, in 2010. And the 2012 film *Cloud Atlas*, based on the book by best-selling author David Mitchell, was highly acclaimed. We also see expanding conversation about the afterlife and near-death experiences that has bridged both communities of skeptics and believers as a result of best sellers such as Dr. Eben Alexander's *Proof of Heaven: A Neurosurgeon's Journey into the Afterlife* and Anita Moorjani's *Dying to Be Me: My Journey from Cancer, to Near Death, to True Healing*. Dr. Wayne Dyer's final book, *Memories of Heaven: Children's Astounding Recollections of the Time Before They Came to Earth*, coauthored with Dee Garnes and published just after Dyer's death in 2015, is filled with children's spontaneous recollections relating to our ongoing existence, and has two sections devoted to reincarnation. These films and books, along with many others, not only demonstrate the general public's hunger to learn more about the mysteries of our existence but also show our increased openness to expanding our beliefs.

Whether a client is somewhat of a skeptic, a confirmed believer, or something in between, he/she does not have to believe in reincarnation or any other particular belief to have a successful regression session. What I have found is that, as long as the mind is open to possibilities, anyone can be a good past life regression candidate. People from widely different spiritual traditions and belief systems and from different cultures and parts of the world have been successful in recovering past life memories.

Of course, there are many people who believe we live only one human lifetime. In this case, the stories elicited by this therapeutic approach can serve as marvelous symbolic metaphors for the issues and situations being faced at the present time. Even if one believes these memories are not true past life experiences, they function as representative stories and are equally as effective in resolving current issues. Whether uncovering "real" past lives or not, past life therapy has helped many people resolve issues and get past blocks that were resistant to other conventional approaches.

———

Past life therapy was once dismissed as a "New Age gimmick" within the counseling community, and it has now become more and more accepted as a credible and effective therapeutic approach that is being used alongside conventional tools. In my own practice, close to 90 percent of my clients have retrieved past life memories on their first try. Considering the fact that we are using a very light level of hypnosis—closer to a gentle, relaxed state that allows the client to easily talk with me throughout the session—it would be misleading to write off these results as coming from the power of suggestion. So let's look a little closer at the theory behind this therapeutic discipline.

Modern past life therapy is based on the premise that we are all eternal beings who experience physical life on earth in a series of human bodies and their associated personalities. As eternal souls, we carry forward the experiences and lessons learned from one human lifetime to another. On a deeper or soul level, we are involved in choosing aspects of each life as a means of expanding our experiences, learning the lessons we have set out for ourselves, and continuing our ongoing involvement with various other souls with whom we are strongly connected.

As humans, we unconsciously carry forward experiences, attitudes, and relationship dynamics from prior lives into our current lifetimes. Many times this is beneficial, as in cases in which we have a natural gift or seem to master a new skill or area of study as if we already knew it. At other times, traumatic experiences, like a violent death or loss of a loved one, are left unresolved, relationships are left unhealed, or attitudes and decisions that are detrimental to our current life may be carried forward from a past lifetime.

In addition to resolving these experiences from the past that are blocking our progress and happiness now, past life work is also very useful in bringing forth strengths and positive experiences from prior lifetimes that can actually enhance our current abilities and confidence. Our prior personalities can help us reach our full potential now!

Past life therapy is becoming more and more accepted in the mainstream as an extremely useful therapeutic tool. It can be a rapid way to bring up and resolve issues in one or two sessions that might otherwise take many months or years of traditional counseling to address. And it can be useful as well for those who would not otherwise consider themselves in need of counseling or therapy services: people who want to expand their experience, draw upon inner wisdom, and connect with loved ones across the ages.

This work can lead to significant transformations in how you view yourself and the world: people often come away with a greater realization of the eternal nature of their being, their connection to others, and a closer experience of the love-filled energy that underlies all life. There is nothing like going through your own death, realizing that your awareness continues past the existence of your physical body, and finding yourself reunited with loved ones and the incredible love that permeates eternal existence. It is a much less traumatic way to have a near-death experience that transforms your view on life than having to actually experience a serious illness or life-threatening accident.

What Issues Can Be Addressed with Past Life Therapy

Some of the significant areas in which past life therapy has traditionally been used are the following:

- Troubling behavior and attitude patterns that have persisted over time despite attempts to change.

- Relationship dynamics that seem to have a life of their own (e.g., intense attraction/aversion to another person, or deep-seated issues that defy resolution).

- Phobias: intense fears, such as fear of heights or fear of water, that do not seem connected to an experience in the current life.

- Some chronic physical ailments, sensations, and pains.

- Dominant attitudes or emotions that seem to persist throughout one's life (e.g., depression, anxiety, or negativity).

Past life therapy also can focus on more positive past life experiences in addition to going after traumatic or troubling memories. This can be an exciting and rewarding avenue when applied to areas such as these:

- Accessing strengths and accomplishments from prior lifetimes that can be brought forward to increase confidence in the present.

- Reexperiencing a happy, successful lifetime, which can bring a sense of balance and peace when undergoing difficult times.

- Clarifying direction and life purpose by viewing one's blueprint for this lifetime.

- Finding prior lifetimes shared with current loved ones, bringing a great sense of reassurance that we are indeed never parted from those we love.

- Accessing the wisdom, peace, and guidance that are available from the "interlife," the spiritual realm we inhabit between physical lifetimes on earth, where our higher mind and/or spiritual guidance can assess our progress and give direction to our current lifetime.

- Strengthening the clarity of the spiritual nature of our existence.

Of course, not all problems and issues are rooted in experiences from prior lifetimes. It is important to distinguish when we have a current life issue that needs to be addressed directly through other means. This includes assessing whether there is a biochemical imbalance that needs to be addressed—for instance, with antidepressants or antianxiety medications.

Even if you don't resonate with any of the aforementioned issues, and you are simply curious and wonder if you've lived before, then something may be calling to you to give past life therapy a try. It is a wonderful way to expand your definition of who you are and what life on this planet is all about. It's an exciting adventure into discovering your true nature.

In a typical session, I have found that, for most people, past life memories are actually fairly close to the surface; we typically are just too distracted in our normal daily lives for the memories to surface, or we don't give them much credence when they do. When I work with clients, a level of relaxation that feels similar to a meditative state is usually very effective in allowing past life memories to emerge, and I do this by using a hypnotic process that deeply relaxes the client. Quite simply, it is a way of entering a very relaxed state whereby your memory is enhanced and the limits and constraints of the logical, conscious mind can be bypassed, and we gain access more easily to the unconscious mind. In this state it is easier to call up images, symbols, and thoughts we have forgotten consciously, just as we do when we're dreaming. In this hypnosis, however, the client is not asleep. Other than being very relaxed and focused on inner images and feelings, the client remains aware of what is going on around him/her; after all, the client and I are conversing throughout the session as I guide him/her through the process.

A valuable component of each of my sessions is that I ask clients to tap into their higher guidance. What do I mean by this? I typically invite a client to imagine that a very wise and loving being is coming forward to be with him/her. This wise being can take a variety of forms for the client: most often we see deceased relatives or an angelic spiritual guide; at times it's an animal or just a ball of color. I can't say for sure what we are plugging into; perhaps the client is linking into his/her own higher mind or consciousness, perhaps it's a deep sense of intuition, or he/she is actually accessing a spiritual source. One way or another, the client seems to connect with a wiser, deeply understanding, and very loving energy (maybe the divine) that is often able to give important advice, offer guidance, or share profound spiritual truths. This can be key in helping the client integrate understandings from the prior lifetime into his/her current awareness.

How to Use This Book

All the client stories in the book follow a similar structure. I briefly introduce the client and his/her reason for seeking past life work. We then go into the body of the actual regression, which unfolds pretty much the way it does in session: sometimes full of twists and turns and unexpected outcomes. I typically guide the client through his/her death in the prior life, and then we process that lifetime's experiences from a place of higher guidance and understanding. We move toward integration by examining the lessons from that lifetime, how the events and lessons relate to the client's current life. What I have found is that there is an incredible amount of wisdom, learning, and intrinsic value contained in these stories. Each individual's higher guidance becomes universal wisdom that can truly benefit all of us.

The case studies are fascinating and, I will admit, entertaining, like a Hollywood costume drama or historical fiction that you can't put down. What is still amazing for me is the amount of detail that many clients can recall and the deep emotions that can be felt across the ages and relived in the present. These stories have profoundly moved me, and I believe they are inspiring anecdotes that can be a source of self-exploration. These case studies were chosen because their inherent life lessons have a universal and common message, whether in your own life or in the life of someone you know. I invite you to make this an even more engaging process by considering some of the questions for reflection, called "Expanding Your Perspective," that you will find at the end of each chapter.

Of course, this is purely optional, and I don't blame you if you just want to go to the next interesting story. You can always come back later when you have more inclination and time to examine how you might integrate some of the information from these stories. If you're serious about increasing your own past life awareness, it can be helpful to use a journal to record your thoughts and answers to the questions in "Expanding Your Perspective" sections, and then review for past life clues you may discover. My hope is that these stories will prove to be stimulating and open your awareness to the vast potential of your consciousness. When you finish each case study, you can ask yourself these general yet insightful questions: If this were my story, what lessons, conclusions, or beliefs would I draw from it: the same ones as the client or different ones? What meaning would this story have for me personally?

Chapters 8, 13, 17, and 21 do not focus on a specific client's case study; rather they offer a deeper look at four key reasons that many clients seek past life therapy: past life influences on their emotions, relationships, physical bodies, and spirituality. These chapters serve as a jumping-off point followed by case studies that illustrate each particular arena, so if you just have to find out more about how a past life can affect your current relationships (Chapter 13), then feel free to jump ahead if you need to. But I highly recommend that you come back and read the rest, because each story really does have something unique to offer!

Lastly, the appendices offer some of my recommended resources and information if you want to delve deeper. I invite you to be curious and educate yourself about past life therapy. Once you do, you will undoubtedly discover how expansive and deep the subject really is. As I mentioned in the introduction, my purpose in writing this book is to not only demystify past life therapy and demonstrate its effectiveness as a therapeutic tool that can help all kinds of people live happier and more fulfilled lives, it is also to expand mainstream awareness of the eternal nature of our existence. Your curiosity and open mind are the first steps toward achieving that purpose.

———

Although most clients take their regression experience at face value, from time to time I do have clients who decide to do some research to validate the information that came up for them. The next chapter, "3501, I'm OK," is probably one of the most illustrative of a prior life bleeding over into the current life, and of the client's being able to research and validate his past life memories. I think it's a good place to start. It's an intense story with some strong language, but it gives you an idea of how vividly the client was reexperiencing the events of a prior lifetime.

CHAPTER 2

3501, I'm OK

JONAH DECIDED TO consult me a couple of months after having a troubling dream, because he wanted to know if it was real. An additional clue came when he had passed out in the back of a friend's car after a heavy night of drinking. He suddenly came to his senses repeating the phrase "3501, 3501, I'm OK!" over and over. His buddy thought maybe it was an address where Jonah wanted to go. Jonah himself admitted he had no clue what "3501" meant. It became a standing joke between the two of them.

Sometime later, 3501 reappeared in another vivid and disturbing dream. I'll let Jonah's own words from an e-mail describe it:

> In this dream I am a soldier in Vietnam. I am in a special operations unit; I am alone, my unit members are dead or missing. The commander of the NVA [North Vietnamese Army] we are fighting calls out to me, he tells me to come out, that I am outnumbered and it is a matter of time before I am found. I am out of ammo and wounded. He tells me if I come out he will kill me quickly and allow me to die like a man.
>
> I come out and he makes me look at him, he then shoots me in my groin. The pain is very severe . . . I feel a sharp pain on my forehead. He shot me again! I feel a slight thump behind

my right ear. I am then on the ground. I can see several NVA soldiers around me but I can't speak and I can't move. It's like I am asleep, but I can see them. I feel no pain, just a weird cloudy sensation.

As I am waking up from the dream, I yell, "What is my name, who am I?" A voice tells me my name, and it tells me I was killed in 1970 in Vietnam. It tells me to remember 3501. I argue with it. I tell it I was born in 1972. It says: "That is enough time." When I woke up I couldn't remember what my name was but I felt the back of my head. Behind my ear I have a small indentation exactly where I was shot in my dream. I also have what feels like a small indentation ending in a groove down my forehead on the left side of my head, exactly where I was shot in my dream.

I had this dream the morning of Veteran's Day.

As you might expect, in addition to wanting to verify the dream, Jonah was also looking for the explanation of 3501, which seemed to be so important. He also noted that, since having the dream, he had been getting information about people from "a voice" that he considered, in his words, "rather crazy." The voice would tell him things about his friends, things he didn't otherwise know. When he checked this out, to his surprise, the friends would verify the accuracy of the information. Jonah shared with me that he was pretty skeptical himself about even keeping our appointment. But just when he was going to call to cancel, he saw a license plate with the numbers 3501. Because of that synchronicity, he was convinced he needed to keep the appointment.

It seemed apparent to me that we were approaching a memory that, although very traumatic, was close to the surface and ready to emerge. The dream was very intense and lifelike for Jonah. The physical manifestations on his body that seemed to relate to the injuries in the dream sounded like the kind of past life carryovers that are sometimes seen when a prior life is impinging on the present. It's as if the unfinished business brings some markers along into the current life as a tangible reminder of what happened. Also, in cases of a sudden, unexpected, violent death that cuts off a life prematurely, we sometimes see a very quick turnaround into a new lifetime. Jonah seemed like the ideal candidate for a past life regression.

———

I begin the regression by having Jonah lie on the couch while I run through a progressive relaxation technique to put him into a hypnotic state. To ease us into something that looks as if it's going to be pretty dramatic, I first have him go back to a happy childhood memory in this lifetime. I also want to check Jonah's ability to do the work, since he has never participated in any counseling before, nor has he experienced hypnosis. He easily enters a memory when he was two, playing with his father on the grass, trying to grab his keys, feeling a little frustrated because he wants those keys! As I then direct him to return to the dream and lifetime during the Vietnam War, the session becomes a somewhat physical event. Jonah's legs begin to kick out as he lies on the couch, as if he's trapped in something he wants to break out of. He comes into a scene where he is hiding in the bushes and trees. "I don't know where they are!" he says, panic-stricken, and starts crying in intense fear. It is early morning. He and his unit have been sent to assassinate someone: a captain. "But Charlie knew we were coming; we've been ambushed!" He heard shouting and shots fired for a while, but it's quiet now. "I'm all alone; I think they're all dead."

His chest and arms are cold. He is crouched down, hiding in the bushes with his helmet and his rifle, but he has no bullets; they were all used earlier in the fighting. He identifies himself as Corporal Matthews from Albany, New York, a draftee. (He is a little unclear on his first name, but finally comes up with Jonah, his current life's name.) He was selected for Special Forces because he is a good shot. He didn't particularly like the idea of Special Forces and clandestine missions, but he figured maybe it would help him stay alive. He wears a lightning-bolt patch on his shoulder. There are eight men in his unit, led by a Sergeant Woods.

I just have to kill him, he thinks. *I can't leave until I kill him. But I'm fucked! I don't want to be captured!* He begins to sob again in fear and acknowledgment of how little chance he has of escaping this situation.

I give him a break from the intensity by asking what he wanted to do with his life before he got drafted. He settles down physically. "I wanted to be in the NYPD [New York Police Department]," he says proudly. And he talks about the many girlfriends he had back home. He's certainly been playing the field, but one girl named Sally has his particular interest. I ask if Sally seems familiar as someone Jonah knows in his current life, and he identifies her as Jonah's current (second) wife.

"And what about 3501? What does that number signify?" I ask. "That's the last four digits of the serial number on my rifle," he says. "We all have to memorize the serial number. If I have my 3501, then I'm OK." Part of the mystery solved.

We return to the action in Vietnam. Corporal Matthews knows that the target is close by, but he's unable to get a shot at him.

"Drop your weapon!" The target apparently knows English, and he knows where Matthews is. *I think about shooting myself. But I don't want to go to hell; I'm Catholic,* Matthews reflects.

"Come out!"

"I can tell he's scared of me," he observes.

"You're a warrior. If you come out, I promise to kill you. I will shoot you in the head, kill you quickly."

"I think he's lying, but I have zero options. They've got me; I'm screwed." Matthews is desperate. "Everyone else is dead; I'm the last one. They knew we were coming." He lifts his rifle, throws it down, and comes out of the bushes, helmet off and hands on his head.

The NVA officer has a pistol. "Look at me!" he demands. Matthews stares as him, not quite able to believe this is really happening to him. The man shoots him in the groin, laughing.

"Fucking bastard!" Matthews screams. "It hurts, fucker!"

"Look at me!" the NVA yells again.

I need my rifle! Matthews thinks with panic. *The fucker didn't have to shoot me. It HURTS!* There is blood everywhere, but Matthews is still standing. He can't speak from the pain and is looking down at the wound. The NVA shoots at his head but only grazes him. He's still alive.

Fucker! Stop shooting me! I'm going to get my rifle, Matthews thinks. But he can't run. The NVA shoots him again, this time a fatal wound to the head, and he falls to the ground. The NVA walks off. Matthews can hear their voices fading away.

I'm not supposed to die! This was not my plan! Matthews is very angry as we move through his death. As he makes his transition to the spiritual plane, his experience begins to change. He thinks, *This is not so bad; I'm not scared anymore. There's no more anger.* He is surrounded by a thick darkness that obscures his vision but feels quite comfortable. He enters a circle with a shaft of light and sees smoke and clouds.

After a few moments I direct Jonah to go to the place where he can review the life just lived from a higher perspective. As we review that lifetime as Corporal Matthews, the rifle understandably plays an important role. *Don't ever give up your rifle! I shouldn't have surrendered.* These were key thoughts as he died. We often carry over beliefs and decisions from a prior lifetime's death into our current lives. This is why remembering 3501 was so important. Corporal Matthews believed, unrealistically, that if he'd only kept 3501 with him, he would have been safe. Obviously, with no ammunition, even his beloved rifle would not have done him much good.

Jonah identifies the following important personal lessons from that lifetime that are impacting his life today. "I wasn't as good as I thought I was; I should try to be nicer to people. I was very concerned about myself and hurt a lot of people's feelings." He identifies this pattern as playing a role in the failure of his first marriage in his current life, admitting that he did not pay attention to what his wife was saying, being too concerned about his career. And what was that career? Law enforcement—the exact thing that Corporal Matthews so desired to do with his life.

Not too long after the regression session, I received a wonderful e-mail from Jonah describing some research he had done and also filling in more details about his personal history in this lifetime. The similarities are startling, including the military service he had in his current life. He does a nice job of talking about how the regression experience had impacted him. Again I will let his words tell his story directly:

> Some very interesting things have revealed themselves since our session. Of course I tried to find Jonah Matthews but there was no match, however I did find a Joseph Matthews who was killed in 1967 in the Quang Tin province near the DMZ. 3000 Marines were overrun during a battle there. Also Joseph was an assault man who died of small arms fire.
>
> How this information relates to me [Jonah is now speaking of his current lifetime]: During my time in the Army . . . I was surprised to find that I had this ability for warfare . . . I was written up by a two-star General during one exercise because I destroyed a squad of Military Police Officers (twelve soldiers) . . . I never received any specialized training in combat other than basic training. But it came so easy to me . . . I can attribute this to my past life experience and training.
>
> Marine doctrine for troop formation during Vietnam, [was] four teams of eight men with a Sergeant in charge. This is also consistent with my answer [on number of personnel]. Thirty-two men is a lot of people, and I was with seven of them.

This validates to me that I was there. I had no prior knowledge of Marine troop formation. The Army [his current lifetime's experience] uses twelve men in a squad broken up into three four-man teams.

I have a large tattoo on my back that goes from the base of my neck to the bottom of my back. It is a large Tiger [that] seems as if he is looking over his shoulder at you. I had this done before our session. When I saw this picture [of the tiger tattoo] it just clicked with me, and I paid quite a bit of money to have it done. Imagine my surprise when during my research I found that the Special Forces training area was called Tigerland.

During our session I saw . . . that I was in Special Forces. During my research I also found that soldiers became very uneasy when it got quiet. A lot of Nam vets speak about that, that when it got quiet they got very scared. I could hear the terror in my voice [from the recording of the session] when I spoke about how quiet it was.

As for the Jonah/Joseph confusion, I can attribute that to how both names have the same beginning sound, and it was unclear to me at the time. However, the Matthews was clear.

After listening to my session tape and the research I have done on the subject there is no doubt in my mind that I was in Vietnam and died there. It's been very enlightening to say the least. I am now concentrating more on the spiritual side of life, trying to understand what it is that I am to learn in this life . . . As for the dreams, I have not had another since. But I embrace my past and think about it daily.

I had the opportunity to talk with Jonah about ten years after his regression. The Internet can be so helpful in tracking people down! He told me about his experience finding "his" name on the Vietnam Memorial in Washington, D.C., and how intensely emotional that was for him. He had not been able to find out too many other details about Corporal Joseph Matthews, however. He went to the location of Matthews's home of record in Albany, New York, and was disappointed to find that the lot was now vacant. Military records were slim to nonexistent; given that Matthews was in covert operations, we agreed it was unlikely that much information would be forthcoming from that direction.

As for Jonah himself, he was doing very well: he had moved and established his own business and felt that his understanding of his prior lifetime had truly enriched his experience in his current life. This is a wonderful example of how integrating your prior lifetimes can both heal and enhance your current life. Although most names have been changed throughout my writing to protect clients' privacy, Jonah was happy to have Corporal Joseph Matthews's name used as is, in the hope that someone who knew him might come across this story. If that does occur, please contact me, and I will arrange for you and Jonah to get in touch. It would be a fitting end to a very moving story.

ESSENTIAL TRUTHS UNCOVERED

* Finding balance between our relationships and career pursuits.
* Practicing kindness and thoughtfulness of others' well-being.
* Carrying forward talents and aspirations that can be realized in a future lifetime.

EXPANDING YOUR PERSPECTIVE

Recurring dreams and dreams that are very vivid and stay with us long after being dreamt are fertile ground for past life work. Very often it could be past life material that is emerging from our un-conscious in the dream state. At times these dreams can be quite troubling—children's night terrors, for example, or Jonah's dream described above—but not always.

Do you have a recurring dream or one that was particularly vibrant and memorable? Could this be a past life memory coming through? Can you identify the time period, place, or maybe even names? One way to harness the potential of your dreams is to suggest to yourself before going to bed that you would like to get more details during each dream. Plant the idea in your unconscious that you are going to learn your name, the date, and the location in the dream, or see people who were important to you in that lifetime. Be sure to have a journal close at hand when you wake up! If we don't write our dreams down immediately, we often quickly lose important details. Having a journal nearby is also a way of letting your unconscious know that you're serious about pulling up past life material. Be pa-tient and don't give up if you don't get results right away; it may take time. Dreams have the potential to convey important messages from our unconscious if we bother to listen and pay attention.

CHAPTER 3

Weighty Issues

CAROL WAS A TALL, impressive woman in her early fifties, admittedly rather heavy, but she carried it well on her large frame. She was very successful professionally but shared that she had struggled with a body concern, feeling too big and too heavy her entire life. She said that her biggest period of weight gain occurred while living in Europe. Carol expressed a fear that the weight issue was getting worse over time, rather than better. She had tried Weight Watchers, exercise, and acupuncture, among other things, with no result.

"I am fifty-one years old, and this just isn't working for me," she related in an e-mail. Carol had read several of Dr. Brian Weiss's books and attended a large group workshop with him in the past, so she was familiar with how effective a past life regression could be in addressing enduring issues that hadn't responded to other approaches. She wanted to see if an individual session would help her break the hold that overeating had on her life. The phrase that resonated for her to describe how she felt was "always feeling too big, and totally disconnected with my body." We used this as her entry point for a prior life.

———

As I guide Carol to relax and connect to a past lifetime, she reports experiencing only darkness, alternately describing it as being like thick smoke and then like being in a fog. Black and red colors swirl around, and she feels slightly nauseated as she continues to float through an increasing murkiness. I try another approach, instructing her to imagine a hallway full of doors, with one particular door that is beckoning to her. This successfully moves her past the resistance as she finds a dark mahogany door with tarnished brass fittings, which opens easily into another scene.

"I'm standing on a wood floor; it's austere, clean," she begins. "It's on the second floor; I can see a window with crisp white curtains, a sink, a single bed . . . I'm in a boardinghouse." Once Carol enters the lifetime, she has excellent recall of detail.

I have her focus on herself, starting with the shoes she's wearing. This is a common technique to help the client more strongly connect with the prior body and personality. She is wearing "black, strappy shoes, white stockings, a blue dress like you see in *Alice in Wonderland*." She identifies herself as a girl about fifteen years old with thick, brown, wavy hair. "I work there," she explains, "cleaning and organizing." She describes it as pleasant but austere. "Shaker-y or Amish-y," she says. "I like cleanliness and orderliness, though," she continues, and says that she's happy there.

Since she reports being on the second floor, I instruct her to go downstairs to the kitchen. She describes going down the service stairway at the back of the house. It's narrow, with redwood paneling and a thin railing. On the way down, I prompt the girl to focus in on a date and location. She identifies the date as the early 1900s, maybe 1916. She's in San Francisco or possibly slightly to the north, in Marin County. The building is all redwood, and it's a busy place with lots of visitors. It turns out the boardinghouse is run by her family.

In the dining room, there is a sideboard with a big table. Many more people than just the family are fed here, she explains. She describes the furnishings as "somewhat ornate, Victorian-ish, maybe European antiques."

I want to probe into her family relationships. We focus on her mother first, and she describes their relationship as comfortable if not close; her mother is "businesslike, not beloved, just efficient, matter-of-fact." She is a large woman wearing an apron that is very clean, and a cap. Mother and daughter cook and clean for the boarders and the family.

Her father is not present at the moment, but she describes him as wearing an ill-fitting tweed suit, a white shirt, and a bowler hat. He apparently is gone quite a bit on some kind of business, and she doesn't see him that often. There is no significant emotional connection, and she feels quite neutral about him. The family also includes a younger brother who is about ten years old. She does not report any strong emotional connection to him, either.

We jump forward, looking for a significant event in that lifetime. The young woman is now about twenty-three years old and is in a large city, which appears to be New York. She describes herself as wearing professional attire: a long shirtwaist dress with puffy shoulders, fitted arms, and a hat. She is working as a journalist or professional writer, is proud of her position, and is quite comfortable in her situation. Although single, she is not lonely. She describes herself as fairly attractive and says that "people are drawn to me." She feels more connected here and finds her work extremely meaningful.

Advancing again, she is now much older, describing herself as tall and thin, with white hair and glasses. She still resides in an apartment in New York City. She's sitting in a chair near the fireplace, sharing stories about her life. "I'm known," she says proudly, "and they want to know 'How did you do it as a woman?' so they can do it too—the writing." She describes her life focus to have been her work. Writing was her passion, and "I broke a barrier!" she says.

However, she admits that she did not have any strong emotional connections in this lifetime, and on her final day she dies alone in her room. Her final thoughts, nonetheless, are of satisfaction with her life: "I did something of consequence and opened doors for others."

Not what we had expected. What happened to the weight issue? Although the lifetime revealed in a session usually addresses the issue the client poses, from time to time we do get something entirely different. When this happens, the lifetime typically addresses another concern—sometimes a concern the client admits later was more important to see than what he/she initially asked about. At times during sessions I feel a little like a detective solving a mystery as I work to ferret out the impact of the lifetime and how it relates to the client's question. In this case the lifetime certainly seemed to resonate with Carol's current focus on her professional career. Since there was time left in the session, we agreed it would be worthwhile to explore whatever lifetime might have set up the dynamics for the writer's life when she chose career over personal connections.

—————

Moving into another lifetime, Carol finds herself in a large square building paneled in dark wood, ornately carved, with expensive railings. There is a big open space on the inside with a catwalk-like structure around it. A big staircase made of cherrywood leads up with a severe pitch to a second floor or mezzanine.

Once again Carol describes herself as a young woman of about fifteen years. She wears a heavy velvet dress and black slippers. She is extremely thin and claims that she is physically uncomfortable, perhaps not well: she experiences nausea and has a head that feels very full. As we explore this further, she identifies it as emotional pressure. "I'm fearful; I'm flitting around, but mainly to avoid people. I have a churning in my stomach. There are a lot of people here, but I stay away," she explains.

We identify the time period as sometime in the Renaissance, and she and her family appear to be in France, as her family is French-speaking. Her family is wealthy, but once again she feels a lack of emotional connection among the family members. She actually says, however, that she likes her parents. She describes her father, who wears a powdered wig, as a good, safe, warm person. "I feel OK with him; he likes me." She sees her mother as wearing a very fancy gown. "She likes me but doesn't pay much attention to me," the young girl claims.

As we move forward, a man enters the picture. He has dark hair tied back in a ponytail. "He's beautiful," she says, "but I'm not attracted to him. He causes discomfort, pressure." It appears he wants to obtain her parents' money and prestige by marrying her, but she feels he's not really interested in her as a person. The details are sketchy, but it appears that they eventually have a disagreement that escalates into a physical assault that ends in her death. "I die badly," she cries. She feels a wound in the area of her ribs, "a huge something, in the center of me . . . He ran me through with a big spear, impaled me on the door, and he got away with it!"

As she dies, she describes feeling a huge loss of self and a weight over her heart. "I trusted him because my parents did, and then he killed me. I was just a pawn for him, totally expendable. It was that way also with my mom. Nobody cared that deeply for themselves or for me. Posturing, politeness, mattered more."

As we review the two lifetimes with the help of her higher guidance, some important lessons are revealed, and we do finally get the connection to Carol's weight issue. By being large, she was buffering herself from once again being treated as a beautiful but unimportant adornment. It's not surprising that living in Europe again in her current life stimulated a need to protect herself from a similar fate.

Carol sums up the lessons from the lifetime of the journalist as follows: "It doesn't mean you have to have family and love to have a worthwhile life. It can be worthy and fulfilling without deep connections; they are an option. However, it could have enriched the life even more with deep connections." The French Renaissance lifetime centered more on her inability to get over her sense of betrayal. "I couldn't forgive my parents for not taking care of me; how could they have let that happen? Politics and posturing mattered more than people. But we are all just people despite our extraordinary trappings."

Carol's work in the spiritual realm centered on letting go of her sense of betrayal, finding forgiveness, and connecting with a deep sense of love from her spiritual guidance. She was able to understand why deep personal connections felt so important but also conflicting in her current life. She gained further insight on how she used her weight now to disconnect from people and to avoid physical touch, to create barriers for safety. I suggested further work on connecting with her body, feeling safe within it, and enjoying movement and exercise as part of her healing.

———

Carol returned to do another regression about six weeks later. She wished to work on that all-important issue of self-worth and self-esteem. She had come to recognize that self-doubt had been creeping in as she attempted to write a scholarly book related to her career activities.

Carol had made some important connections in the intervening time and filled me in on more of her personal history. She described her mother as "needy and feeding off disaster" and recalled her adolescence as being very unhappy. In addition to her size/weight issues, she was upset that her parents were "consumed with each other. I felt like an outsider; my parents didn't think I was important or worthy." Carol believed that her father in this lifetime was the same soul as her father in the French Renaissance lifetime, and there were many parallels between the family dynamics in the two lifetimes.

———

We once again start the regression with Carol floating in smoke and darkness. After a little work to settle her into a lifetime, just as before, her memories become quite solid. Her first image is of a thick Persian rug on the floor, then a desk, and she identifies the room as a home library with books all along the walls. There's a fireplace in the room, and, looking out the window, she sees a manicured lawn, a meadow, and a forest behind it. She believes she is once more in France.

I ask her to focus on herself, and she says that she's female. She's wearing a very full dress with many petticoats and black, heeled, slipper-type shoes with a strap and a button. She describes herself as having "a pretty face with sharp features; very fair, a pointy nose, and light brown hair done up stiffly." Her ability to recall detail continues. "My dress has big sleeves, white inner lace, a coral bodice. I have thin, long hands." She is married, twenty-eight years old, and then she surprises me by saying, "Benjamin Franklin and Thomas Jefferson are around!" At the moment, however, she is alone in her home. "Many people use the library," she notes, remarking, "it's comfortable."

We move forward and join a dinner party in a very ornate room in her house. There are a lot of men in attendance, no children, and just a few other women. "It's serious, not just social. We're thinking of something . . ." She ponders this. The participants are standing around, talking, with quite a sense of importance. "Many points of view are expressed, understanding from many perspectives. It's not usual for women to be involved, but they see it's necessary for the wisdom of it."

I ask her to look for a significant person in the room. She identifies a colleague: it's Benjamin Franklin. His mission: How do you build a constitution? "We are sharing ideas on forming a new country with all people . . . what has to be in place afterwards . . . how to do it so everyone's included, even women." She describes the conversation as very engaging, very practical and down-to-earth: "sensible, not hypothetical."

We also identify her husband. He is tall, dark-haired, about thirty-five years of age. "He's very likable and honest. We have a lot, but we don't see ourselves as privileged. We're trying to make a better world, yet we're a little oblivious to the fact that we have so much," she reflects. "It's an easy relationship." She continues: "We're friends, we value each other, and he's a nice companion."

As I direct Carol to move forward to the next significant event, she loses contact with the lifetime. As we move into processing the amount that we have seen, it appears we had hit upon the important aspects of that lifetime.

"It was a resting life, not difficult," she reflects. "There was the pleasure of companionship, the stimulation of intellectual pursuits." A key message emerges: "All lives are valuable for some reason; the lessons can come more gently. We're all valuable. There's a place for each of us in the universe; all our contributions are needed; one opinion is not enough." This was quite important for her to have revisited the experience of being valued, being listened to, having her opinions solicited.

In this session, Carol's spiritual guidance gives her a number of practical suggestions about taking life a little more lightly. "Something doesn't always have to be revealed," her inner voice tells her. "Let go of expectations; be in the experience." She is also given a number of very practical suggestions to help her writing. "Stay away from TV and distractions; use music; find the artist within. Trust it's there, and craft it."

————

I have to admit it was fun to have a historical figure like Benjamin Franklin show up in a regression, especially since it's quite unusual for big names to make their appearance. It was fascinating to follow Carol's story as she described the dynamic within what we today would call a "think tank."

That aside, this regression series does a wonderful job of illustrating how our patterns evolve over lifetimes. If we follow this chronologically, we see the plight of the female figure in the Renaissance lifetime: feeling unloved, treated as a dynastic pawn, and dying a terrible death at the hands of her betrothed. In contrast, the woman in the Franklin lifetime finds herself being treated with respect as her opinions on how to build a new society are being solicited by the men around her. And she experiences a wonderful connection with her life partner. Then the more recent lifetime chronologically, which we saw in the first regression, shows a woman who breaks the barriers on her own, living a single but very professionally fulfilled lifetime. A step forward in her self-actualization, perhaps at the expense of some closer human connections. It appears that, in her current life, Carol is now attempting to put the icing on the cake: she is integrating an accomplished professional career, marriage, and parenthood, and she continues to work on feeling relaxed in closer relationships.

ESSENTIAL TRUTHS UNCOVERED

* Balancing connection to others with the need for self-actualization.
* Understanding that we are all valuable and everyone's contribution is needed.
* Pushing the boundaries of cultural expectations and limitations.
* Realizing that we are all equal despite the trappings of wealth and position.

EXPANDING YOUR PERSPECTIVE

Self-definition versus connection can be a difficult and delicate balance for many of us. For women in particular, the indoctrination by cultural and/or family expectations to define ourselves through our relationships—our spouses, our children, our friendships—is a very strong message. It may be subtler now in today's Western culture, but it certainly hasn't disappeared. In some cultures around the world, it is still fundamental to a woman's worth.

Whether you are male or female, how are you managing the balance in your life between defining yourself and being connected with others? Does having close personal connections feel a little unsafe or unfamiliar to you? Do you have a chronic issue, like Carol and her weight, that serves to create distance from other people and provides a buffer from that challenging arena of relationships? What would happen if you shifted your focus away from that issue and dealt with the relationship challenge more directly? Are there adjustments you would like to make in that balance between your self-definition and connectivity? How could you go about doing that so that you, too, can realize greater fulfillment in multiple areas of your life? These are rich questions to explore in contemplation and journaling.

CHAPTER 4

A Walk with the Medicis

IT REALLY SHOULDN'T come as a surprise that most past life stories do not take us back to lifetimes in which the client is an important historic figure. In the scheme of things, there have been millions of average, everyday people over the centuries compared to a very small number of people whose names were significant enough to endure in our history books. However, as we've seen, from time to time historic figures do show up, and it's always a fun and, at times, surprising experience when this occurs.

In one particular case, my client, Raja, was a young man in his late twenties who was born and educated in India. He was quite forthcoming with his introductory e-mail to me, and described himself as follows:

> I did well academically in primary, middle, and high school, and at law school in India. I often took on projects others were reluctant to take on . . . I was never afraid to swim upstream to achieve what I set out to do. I was involved in a number of extracurricular activities—playing the tabla [a South Asian musical instrument], karate, tennis, and sailing, and participated in a number of debating, student government and committee related activities . . . I have travelled a fair bit—and have spent

time in parts of India, Kashmir, Italy, UK, Thailand, Germany, Czech Republic, Switzerland, Belgium, Portugal, Austria, Spain, France, Netherlands, Egypt, Kenya, Hong Kong, New York and parts of the US.

Raja was now confronting taking the bar exam in the United States, and he was also facing some serious questions about his current legal career.

"One of the primary reasons I chose to become an attorney," he wrote, "was to be able to touch many people's lives in different ways and help ameliorate them, if at all, in whatever way possible." He was beginning to question if he was truly able to fulfill this objective in his current situation—feeling the pull of profit and materialistic motivations in his current firm—or even if the law itself was the right line of work for him. He was hoping that past life regression might assist him in making some important career decisions and in finding out what the next step would be in fulfilling his purpose of helping others. I looked forward to working with this thoughtful, dynamic, and highly accomplished "Renaissance man" even before I met him.

––––––––

Raja's first impression is of red leather shoes with gold embroidery. He is wearing a very ornate, maroon-red robe made of heavy, soft fabric that falls all the way to the floor. It has full, long sleeves with slits in the side, a high collar, and gold embroidery, with gold buttons on the cuffs. Under the robe he wears a frilly white shirt, and he has a skullcap on his head. At first he describes himself as a fairly young man with fair skin and a "soft face with pronounced features." However, he soon realizes there is another person, a middle-aged man with a beard, dressed similarly, and that he is this latter figure. He is in discussion with the younger man.

The men are outdoors on a green lawn, with a huge manor on top of the hill behind them. He sees many hills and feels the warmth of a summer evening. He identifies the location as somewhere in Italy.

"I'm extremely rich," he observes. "I feel responsible for others. . . .
I set up institutions of higher learning. . . . It's the mid-Renaissance,"
he explains. "My manor is full of paintings, art—tons of it! And I
would like to share it with others."

To gain a better picture of his personal life situation, I direct him
to his most recent meal. He sits at the head of a long table with an
older woman, attended by a number of servants. They are eating
fruit, particularly grapes. "We don't like meat," he comments. The
woman is short, with a small face and brown eyes, and she wears a
very ornate gown. "She's older than me," he comments. "Not my wife,
but protective of me. An aunt or the like, and she is very learned,
although she speaks little."

His attention moves back to the art. "As a child I was always surrounded by art: huge paintings on the walls. And I desired the same
for myself. This is just one of my manors . . . I grew up in a bigger city,
in Firenze [the name for Florence in Italian]."

"We were traders," he continues. "And we made a lot of money.
We were exposed to different art, history, and cultures. We lived
very differently from the average person; we had many visitors, were
surrounded by music and art. We commissioned art and fueled the
growth of the art movement. We listened to new forms of thought—
philosophy, astrology, and the like.

"Everyone was happy and content. I wanted to create institutions
for others to learn so they could appreciate and savor it too!" When
prompted for a name, "Fellini Medici" was his answer. The Medici
family was one of the wealthiest and most important families in Italy
during the Renaissance. Raja describes a family house in Firenze that
was turned into offices, shaped like two capital *L*'s put together, with
three floors and a fountain. (This would be the now-famous Uffizi
Gallery.)

Our Renaissance man describes with enthusiasm the rapid
growth he has helped foster. "It's reaching the pinnacle of expression.
It's so exciting and fulfilling—I want it to last longer, so others can

be a part of it! My days are so full of artists and performers and state dignitaries. It's totally engaging." He mentions the Italian painter Botticelli and that he knows him well. He also mentions a daughter, "very beautiful and talented," who is identified as Raja's current sister. We are not able to focus in on the figure of a wife.

I ask Signor Medici to move forward in that lifetime to a significant event or when something changes. "The house is quiet, empty." But it is not due to a crisis; he has made a choice to take a break. He's in his fifties now, turning very philosophical, and he wants to study more. "I know people think incorrectly about the world. The earth is round, the planets revolve around the sun, and there may be other life on other planets!" he exclaims. "I have a telescope, but it's not powerful enough. I'm looking for a way out, a way to connect with what else is out there. It could be familiar to me. Few others can relate to me on this; they think I'm mad," he frets.

Signor Medici expounds on his vision and mission. "People need to see and understand what is greater, what is beyond—not just daily life. Everything we do has greater effect than we know. Mind and actions are creating. Energy constantly changes. Everything is in motion, down to the tiniest particles. Time comes and goes.

"For me, it's a journey. Maybe one or two others think like me. I know many civilizations have known this truth. But the time is not right now. I can help through schools—special ones—the central underlying theme being interconnectedness, being in tune with the energy. I can't set it up yet, even today. But the time is coming soon."

Death comes peacefully to Signor Medici. He is much older, with a white beard. He is sitting in a chair, his leather diary in his hands, filled with diagrams and text, the important truths he has discovered in his life of exploration and study. His final thoughts have to do with "balancing energy and understanding. I'm on a path; major milestones are coming so close." In his final moment, he gets some glimpses into future incarnations, with a realization of the connections that exist between lifetimes.

As we look at the lessons from that inspired past life, Raja rapidly lists a number of them: to share, to teach, to learn, to write; to help people; to travel—see different places and cultures; to spend time with learning—noting that there's always more to learn; to know what's right and wrong; to balance individuals and situations.

Raja notes that his love of antique books in the current lifetime springs from his days as a Medici, where learning was foremost.

As we inquired of Raja's spiritual guidance, particularly in regard to his current career questions, he was told, "Law is only a stepping-stone, meant to build a base of higher learning. Don't worry about the means; you will always be taken care of," he is reassured. He is also encouraged to go to Asia. "The surge is eastward," he is advised. "There is a lot of ancient wisdom there. Be around it even if you don't understand it! You can be a participant there, but only a spectator if you are here."

———

And, indeed, later contact with Raja showed that he had followed his guidance and moved to Asia. Five and a half years after the regression session, he sent the following in an e-mail:

Post the regression, it is amazing the number of times I have been able to put life experiences (past or present) and current reactions to things, people or circumstances into pairs of well-fitting casts and molds. Once paired, I can often choose to do away with the pair altogether, in a way that the space that is left by their expulsion, is neutral, and new experiences . . . are open to being experienced more fully in the present without the past leaning as heavily on it . . . [B]eing sometimes aware of this duality provides a phenomenal opportunity to choose how to move forward in instances where my reaction may otherwise have been largely unconscious . . . [I]t is interesting when I try to infuse . . . feelings or pregnant thoughts into these neutral spaces. These spaces feel like fertile soil in which by

putting thought nutrients, you can enable thoughts or actions
to germinate.

Seeing through the intellectual verbiage, I understand Raja to be
saying that the regression experience has enabled him to make
much more conscious choices, rather than just reacting to people
and circumstances from old programming, and this has created a
great opportunity for personal growth and integration. He believes
the impact to be enduring. Although much of the information that
came up in this regression could be discovered in reading history—
and Raja was indeed well-read and educated—the excitement and
energy in the room and the personality that came out in the session
were unique. I had no doubt that I walked with a Medici for a short
moment in time.

ESSENTIAL TRUTHS UNCOVERED

* Using wealth to benefit others.
* Enjoying learning for its own sake.
* Expanding knowledge to benefit humanity.
* Valuing travel and exposure to different cultures.

EXPANDING YOUR PERSPECTIVE

An interest in particular historical eras can be important clues to
past lifetimes. Certainly living in the center of the Italian Renaissance
must have been a very heady experience, one that Raja seemed to
be continuing in a number of ways in his current life. I had another
client who was fascinated with Czarist Russia and wanted to specifically understand why; she went to a lifetime as the Romanov family's
personal physician shortly before the revolution.

Are there specific times in history that fascinate you in an inexplicable way? Do you love historical novels that focus on a certain time period? Perhaps you're fascinated by the era of the Vikings, the American Civil War, or World War I, or collect antiques from a particular period. List the historical periods that call to you in your past life journal. Allow yourself to imagine what role you might have played in that era. How does this interest enrich your life or your worldview?

CHAPTER 5

Opening New Directions

DEANNE FIRST CAME to see me in 2008. She flew in, rented a car to drive down to my office for her session, and then flew home the same day. It's not unusual for people to travel quite a distance to have a past life session, although others opt for a remote session with a service like Skype or Zoom. This is what initially led me to structure my sessions as onetime, self-contained, two-and-a-half-hour events, rather than a series of shorter sessions. This allows many people to work a session with me into their typically hectic schedules.

The drawback is, we don't have as much opportunity to develop the traditional therapist/client relationship, and most times I know very little about the client with whom I'm working. Unless it's pertinent to the issue the client wishes to explore, I may never even know if someone is married or not. On the other hand, it also means that there are very few assumptions I bring into the session from prior knowledge about the client's life. And I have found that by working at such a deep level with people in regression, I feel that I get to know them on a level that is very intimate and rewarding.

Deanne was an attractive professional woman in her late thirties. She practiced yoga regularly and was devoted to her spiritual exploration and journey. She shared that her father had been an alcoholic and had abandoned the family, leaving her as the oldest child to take care of her brother and her mother. This pattern had endured past her childhood; in fact, it was the reason she came to see me.

"I have a role reversal in my relationship with my mother," she explained. "I feel like I'm in bondage to my mom—a feeling of being energetically tied, with no freedom to be myself in my relationship with her." She was angry and resentful at the burden of her mother's reliance on her, and she could see this reflected in her relationships with other people in her life as well. "Others' neediness causes a tension in me: I'm not free; I have a suffocated feeling in other relationships."

Conventional therapy would look at this dynamic as a classic family-of-origin issue that has been unresolved. It would prescribe going back to the events of Deanne's childhood, exploring what happened to her, the roles assumed by her various family members, the decisions or beliefs about herself and others that she unconsciously developed, and the feelings that were repressed by her at the time. Then she would work to develop new patterns of interaction and new beliefs that are more functional for her. In fact, this is what I would have suggested for her as well, except she already tried that for some years. She still carried that feeling of bondage and lack of personal freedom. So I agreed that it was a good choice to look for that energetic tie with her mother in prior lifetimes. Deanne was able to move quickly into the work.

———

"My feet are bare. I'm standing on the ground; it's dirt," Deanne begins. She describes her feet as "Neanderthal-like; knobby, very tan, big and flat. I seem to be male," she continues. "Hairy legs, lean, short, and stocky. I feel strong." He is wearing some kind of animal skin on his lower torso, with a bare chest. "I have early human features: dark skin, big brown eyes, brown hair—it's wiry and messy."

I ask him to notice his surroundings. They are primitive structures made of mud or dirt, with smooth sides and pitched roofs. It's a little village of maybe a half dozen structures.

"I've come back. There should have been people here. I'm in shock: they've been taken away . . . I didn't get back in time!" He is quite upset.

I ask him to go to a slightly earlier time, before this event, when things are more normal. "I'm with my wife. She looks different than me. She has long black hair, thick and silky. It's tied at the nape of her neck. She's fair-skinned, beautiful. She's pregnant." They have two other small children, and he describes his feelings toward her. "I admire and respect her; there's love and appreciation, deep caring." When I ask if this wife is familiar as someone known in Deanne's current life, she can identify no connection. The "Neanderthal" man describes his activities as mainly hunting for food and other tasks for maintaining daily life. Then I ask him to return to the initial scene of the empty village.

He is bewildered and perplexed, somewhat stuck for a while, until the image of a man on a horse develops. This is someone who looks more like his wife: he wears multiple layers of clothes and rides a big horse; he seems to be of higher status. "These are my wife's people. I feel him looming over me," he says. "They've taken her back; they're not going to let her be with me!" They take the couple's children as well, but one of them, a boy of about two, looks like his father. "They throw him back; they don't want him. I have no choice; I can't influence any of this. I can't see my wife again. But how do I take care of this child?" he laments.

As we move forward in the regression, we see what develops. "I'm happy to have my son. I love him, hold him. We go to a new village— my people. My son is with me. I've accepted our situation. The community will help me with my son." They are enveloped naturally into the community and fit in well. As his son gets older, he is potentially identified as Deanne's brother in her current life.

There is a woman with whom they now live. "I'm grateful and feel indebted to her for taking us in," he says. "But we're a bit of a burden to her. It's not really love, and there's no sexual relationship.

She took us on as a job, sort of, not a real choice. She takes care of my son but is not very loving. But I know he's safe." He describes her as having white hair and is pretty sure this caregiver is Deanne's current mother.

We move forward to a time when his son is about fifteen years old. "He's taller than me, handsome. He's a cross between my wife and me—her fine features, my dark complexion." It's evident that he is very proud of his son and loves him very much. "I'm sad: he's grown. I think he's leaving. But I'm staying with this woman. Let him have his exciting life. I owe her." When I ask how this woman benefits from his staying there unwillingly, he replies, "She's a witch. She takes pleasure in me being trapped and suffering. She's spiteful, mean. I have this sense of obligation and loyalty. I was so desperate for help, I made this agreement. It's like I signed my life away. I would never break my word, but I'm stuck in a purposeless situation for her kicks. She likes having power over me."

As we move forward, he feels his life has become boring and mundane. His son comes and goes, but the periods of absence stretch out longer and longer. He's happy his son is out in the world, but he wishes he could go with him. Not long thereafter, he kills himself by slitting his own throat. *I did it to spite her! You don't have power over me!*—these are his final thoughts.

As we look at that life experience after the death, he expresses considerable regret for poor decisions he has made. "I wish I hadn't handled it that way. I wish I'd had more integrity, more honor, some compassion for her being so nasty," he said. When prompted as to how he could have done things differently, he reflects, "I wish I never made that agreement. I was too hasty; I had a bad feeling about her in the beginning, but I didn't trust my gut. Or I could have renegotiated, explored other options. But I was afraid of the witch's curse." He recognizes there could have been a different outcome. There was a widow with whom he could have been relatively happy if he had abandoned the witch. "She [the widow] would let me come and go," he reflects.

Lessons revealed in that lifetime center on trusting one's gut about people and not acting hastily; using integrity and honor in one's dealings; and saying no in the belief that something better will show up. Gaining a deeper understanding of equality and freedom within relationships was also very significant. We do some clearing work about the energetic bondage that Deanne keeps herself in with her mother, releasing the unspoken agreement that still appears to be in operation. I assign her some homework to practice saying no to her mother's neediness, envisioning a boundary that keeps that neediness at a safe distance. She also agrees to work on reminding herself that her mother's path involves learning to stand on her own two feet.

A final, unrelated image appears to Deanne at the end of the session: a man in a black hat with a wide brim standing outside, looking through a window. "Just because I don't see something doesn't mean it's not going to get me" is the sentence that pops up, along with an overwhelming feeling of vulnerability. It appears that there is more work to do, but that will have to wait for another session.

Three or four days after her session, Deanne sent me an e-mail:

> I had some more clarity on my trip home . . . Some blurry parts filled in a bit. When I went to that second community, I was actually going back to my people. Perhaps the woman was my grandmother or mother. I had left there to be with the black-haired, fine-skinned wife without the blessing of grandmother/mother. When I returned with one of my children and needed help, she held it against me and never forgave me. No compassion . . . "See what you brought upon yourself . . . I told you so" . . . type of thing. Maybe I felt that I couldn't ever leave again to go off with my son, or I was forbidden to do so, or simply felt guilty? ashamed? obligated to stay . . . then had to take care of her . . .
>
> Relationship with my mom has been much better inside of

myself . . . I keep meeting her in spirit and reminding us both that I have given her back responsibility for her life, that I am free, and that she needs to learn to stand on her own two feet. Yesterday, I ended our call abruptly because I spilled something and afterwards didn't have my usual "bad daughter" thought! Now I know where "bad daughter" thoughts come from . . . "bad son/grandson" thoughts! This is so freeing. I love this journey.

About four months later, Deanne flew in again for another session. She said she finally felt free of her mother, between our initial session and some follow-up work she did with a counselor closer to home, in which she focused on standing on her own and finding her own voice. Now she was back to explore another issue.

"What's the point?" Deanne asked in frustration. "I start so many things in life but then give up. Maybe it's fear of failure, but I have the sense it's not important anyway. What's the point of putting out the energy? Nothing is meaningful; nothing is going to come of it!" I suggested we use the statement "Nothing is going to come from my efforts" as her entry point for this regression.

———

"They look like work boots, dark brown, laced," Deanne observes. "I'm wearing linen pants, like a khaki or olive green; a white shirt that's linen or cotton. It's loose and comfortable." As I have her turn her attention to her head and face, she continues: "I have close-shaved hair. My eyes are smallish in a round face. It has lots of character and dimension. A broad nose. I have dark black skin." She identifies herself as a man in his late thirties, healthy and solid: "A good strong constitution," she declares.

He is walking alone along a dirt road in the country. It's sunny and warm, and he can see the golden-colored grass around him. He feels peaceful, at home. He identifies the area as the Midwestern United States; it's the early 1940s. He catches a lift on the tailgate of a beat-up, faded pickup truck.

Arriving at his destination, he is dropped off at a small settlement of shacks made from sapling branches and similar materials. "I've come to visit a little old white lady; maybe she's Hispanic. We know each other. I've been trying to help her. I've come to tell her the news. Someone died. I tried, but I couldn't change the outcome. I am so disappointed, so surprised. I thought I could have an impact!"

It is a young black man who had been raised by the older woman, who has died. "He was a really happy, good-hearted teen," he says. "But he was hanged! They punished him for stealing something."

To gain some background and framework for this situation, I ask to see where our main character lives. He describes himself as well-off, living in a white Colonial-style house with a big porch. There are other homes spread out in the area and lots of big trees. We meet his wife, a lighter-skinned woman, and his daughter. "We're a family; things are good. But I'm preoccupied," he says. "I try to help poor people."

He describes the good works that he performs: "I pick up groceries for the old lady. I take food to people. I look out for them and the care they need. I advocate for them. How could I not? Even small things help. But it's overwhelming at the same time. I'm sad that there's so little I can do, maybe a little guilty that I have more than they do."

We return to the critical event with which the regression started. The younger black man stole some food for the old lady, perhaps under her instructions. "It's a small community, and we thought it would be no big deal, but he took from the wrong people. He was caught by some 'rednecks.' I thought I could use my diplomacy, reason with them. Yet they hung him! No law was involved. We should be beyond that!" He is aghast, outraged, and deeply saddened. The old lady similarly feels horrible and responsible for the young man's death.

"I feel my family's safety is in question, so there's no retaliation for what they [the rednecks] did," he continues. "I'm in shock. Their reaction was so out of proportion! There definitely was a racial component. I feel so naïve, so stupid! I thought we were beyond this. These white rednecks are hateful, angry that we share their land and community."

His self-talk becomes very defeated and negative. "How could I think I could make a difference? What's the point of trying to promote peace among people when there is no consciousness? It's a waste of time and effort to try to reason with them. Nothing I do is enough. I have all these capabilities. I'm healthy, strong; I have money. I should be able to have more impact."

After this event, our philanthropist feels as if he is just going through the motions. He continues his work but sees no real point in it. He dies at home, a very old man, with the drive to make a difference never fulfilled. "I tried to do what I could, but I had only so much influence. It preoccupied me a lot, so I wasn't really present for my family," he reflects in his final moments.

In processing this lifetime, the connection with the "What's the point?" feelings in Deanne's current life is obvious. She reflects that she is doing the same thing now but in a different arena, and she only wants to do things if they're "great." Lessons gained from that prior life include recognizing the need to appreciate more what she has and not be distracted from it by chasing an elusive goal. An intended lesson that she feels she is still struggling with is to realize that "it's good enough to be average. I don't have to be extraordinary; I don't have to be Martin Luther King or Gandhi." Her higher guidance tells her that she did have a previous lifetime, in India, where she did do something extraordinary and made a huge difference. There is something addictive about being that influential, and unhooking from the need to be a "somebody" is an ongoing task she has carried over from that lifetime.

———

It is a little more than a year later when Deanne returns to work on her next step. I'm delighted to hear her report that she now considers her relationship with her mother to be "fantastic!" and that they love spending time together. She also reports that she has gotten over the need to change the world. She is in the midst of a career change to become a holistic health counselor, helping others with nutrition using whole foods and healthy lifestyle counseling. She feels confident in her knowledge and abilities but has come across a roadblock. She is very worried about putting herself in front of people she doesn't know, fearing that she will be harshly judged. We use her phrase "the fear of putting myself in front of people I don't know" as the avenue into the relevant lifetime.

Once again, Deanne is in a male body. He is wearing brown leather thong sandals and a white cotton "wrap" on his lower body—"definitely not pants." He describes himself as having "a Gandhi-like look: a very tan, wiry, bare chest; almost bald, with close-cropped whitish-gray hair at the sides, a round head, and a 'yoga body' that is healthy, strong, and full of energy." He identifies his location as India.

As the opening scene develops, he finds himself on a sunny, hot day, standing outside a small white building with a flat roof and stucco walls. He knows there are people inside, but he's reluctant to go in himself. "I'm unsure what awaits me," he comments hesitantly.

We take an aside to gain some background, and I direct him to where he lives and explore his typical daily activities. His home is a small house of bamboo or grass, surrounded by trees and greenery. "I live alone. It's a simple space. I'm a celibate, monk type." He identifies himself as a teacher of children. "I love doing this," he adds.

Returning to the opening scene, we learn that he has received "a notice on white paper that I must go there." He is concerned about this notice. "Three men are going to question me; they think I did something wrong with the children!" he realizes. "I know these men. But now it's a strangely official situation. I have no idea what the problem is." He feels at a loss but completely innocent of wrongdoing, and he cannot figure out why this is happening.

As he faces his questioners, the situation becomes clear. "I'm being accused of sexual abuse of one of my students!" he exclaims. "They have the wrong guy! I'm very loving toward the kids [they are all boys, he points out in an aside], but it would never even occur to me to do something like that . . . A parent is accusing me, though. I have no opportunity to defend myself. I'm speechless, in 100 percent disbelief." The consequence of the accusation is that he can no longer work with children and must leave the area. "I don't have much ego attachment to convincing them otherwise," he reflects. "I go with the flow."

However, he feels very disappointed and sad. "I really liked my life," he explains. "I liked my home, my work. I'm a good person, a genuine, gentle soul. Just because someone can lie about me, my life is gone. I never even met this parent who has all this power over my life. I have no control. I'm at the mercy of what someone says about me!" He wonders if perhaps this accusation was maliciousness on the parent's part, stemming from jealousy over the child's feelings toward him, his teacher. But he will never know.

Since he must leave, he packs a small sack of belongings and takes a train to another part of India, thinking he can visit a friend who may be able to help him out. However, he is unable to locate his friend and, being quite destitute, resorts to begging for food and a place to sleep in the village. Eventually he just decides to die. "I feel done; I'll leave," he says.

"I feel somehow it's my fault; it should not have happened that way. I should have built another life instead of giving up, a new place to teach, to be of service. Instead I wallowed in despair," he notes as he faces his death.

And this is one of the key lessons we identify from that lifetime: to overcome adversity and not wallow in despair. "To persevere, don't give up, keep being who you are, be confident about who you are, and keep sharing" rings out. The satisfaction of a simple lifestyle and living in the present moment are also identified as influences that have carried through to Deanne in her current life. "I still love simplicity; little things make me happy," she comments. "And I've always been good with solitude."

We look for additional guidance to help her move forward with her new career and to overcome the fear of putting herself out there in the public eye. "You can't control others, but you can trust yourself to be fine no matter what," she is told by the figure of a wise and loving guide. "Ninety-nine point nine percent of the time people are fine, but remember to lock your door at night." A practical, cautionary note. And she is advised: "Gently stretch your comfort zone. You'll get further faster by doing a bit less initially. Don't force yourself through the discomfort; work with it."

———

I think this regression series is a wonderful example of how past life work can unlock dynamics and release patterns of interactions and beliefs about ourselves and the world. It also shows a lovely progression of clearing a key issue, such as Deanne's unhealthy bond with her mother, which then allows other issues to float up and be dealt with. The end result for Deanne was to forge a new, loving relationship with her mom, which led to freeing herself from the need to be extraordinary, which in turn allowed her to move in a new career direction. Her last session helped clear out a further issue that became activated as she moved into more public exposure in that new direction. Dramatic results in moving forward toward expressing her fuller potential in this lifetime were accomplished in three sessions, spread over roughly fifteen months.

ESSENTIAL TRUTHS UNCOVERED

* Overcoming adversity. Never give up, don't wallow in despair.
* Releasing the need to be extraordinary.

* Appreciating what you have. Don't get lost chasing elusive goals.
* Finding equality and freedom in relationships.
* Trusting your gut intuition about people and situations.

EXPANDING YOUR PERSPECTIVE

Many of us share lifetimes again with important others: we may have unfinished business from the past to complete, we may just love being together, or maybe we have agreed to push each other's spiritual growth in less-than-comfortable ways. If you look at your own life and relationships, are there places you suspect some unspoken agreements are operating? What would happen if you were to articulate these unspoken arrangements, at least to yourself, and make a more conscious choice about those that no longer serve you?

As we saw with Deanne's story, by changing her own approach and attitude, the entire dynamic with her mother was transformed. What do you think about the guidance Deanne received that it's good enough to be average or normal, that you don't have to be extraordinary to be a good or helpful person? How would your experience of life change if you adopted this attitude? Are you afraid that you wouldn't accomplish anything? Would being average be enough for you? Or would that relieve some pressure and free you up to discover what you are naturally talented at? Sometimes the heavy demands we put upon ourselves get in the way of discovering and exploring latent talents that will actually help us move in rewarding new directions.

CHAPTER 6

A Case of Writer's Block

CARRIE, A YOUNG Latina in her early twenties, was three papers away from completing her degree at a nearby university. "But I can't write!" she lamented. Each time she would sit down to work on one of the papers she needed to complete, she would have major anxiety— feeling intensely distressed, with pounding heart and sweaty palms.

Carrie had explored possible causes with another therapist, who used more conventional therapeutic approaches. Having been raised in a family with high expectations and educated at Catholic schools, Carrie and her therapist considered performance anxiety as a possible explanation for her recent troubles. They had also investigated the possibility of a latent fear of moving forward after her degree was completed. Neither of these theories seemed to explain her writing dilemma, and the anxiety had continued. Her therapist was familiar with my work and suggested that Carrie might want to explore possible past life precursors. Her story was one of the more awful examples of the brutality that humans can perpetrate upon one another.

"It's dark and cold. I'm scared." This is Carrie's first awareness as she enters the past lifetime. She is wearing thick, rough clothing, brown in color. At first thinking she is male, due to a sense of broad shoulders and large hands, she realizes she is actually a young woman "about twenty years old." The male figure who appears is her guard, "Brutus," someone she immediately identifies as a former boyfriend in Carrie's current life. She is shaking and extremely tired as well as profoundly frightened. She appears to be in a dungeon.

"There's a machine . . . it goes in a circular motion . . . they're keeping it going . . . My hands! They're cutting off my hands with the machine!" The feelings become too intense, and Carrie loses the connection with the memory.

I lead Carrie through some calming breath work, and then we return to the lifetime, watching it as if watching a movie from a comfortable armchair. This is a useful approach in recovering memories that seem too awful to reexperience with their full impact of the moment. Carrie is able to identify that her hands were cut off as a punishment for having written "a paper that I was not supposed to write." Slowly the story unfolds.

"I'm in love with another woman! And I wrote about it," she exclaims. "Brutus found out and told the king."

"Why would the king care?" I ask. "What is your relationship to him?"

"I'm his daughter." However, she describes their relationship as very distant. "He hates me. I wasn't supposed to be born. I'm illegitimate. I live somewhere else [apart from the king]. My mother is dead."

Carrie identifies the place and time as somewhere in Spain in 1581.

"Who is it that you are in love with?" I ask. She describes a young woman with long brown hair. "She's my older cousin. She has the same feelings for me, but from a distance. So I write to her." Carrie is able to identify that the same individual is also her cousin in her current life.

"Brutus is supposed to watch me," she continues. "And he finds the letter. The king orders to put me in this underground room. It's all rock walls. My hands and feet are chained. But first they cut off my hair in the plaza, in front of all the people," she laments. "This is considered a sin, the love of a woman for another woman," she explains. "That's why [sometime later] they cut off my hands, so I can never sin again by writing to her." After this horrible mutilation, she must have received cauterization, because it is not the end of her life.

She is left in the cold, dark dungeon a long time. "Maybe years? I can't get out. Please kill me!" she pleads. Although she knows there is another woman imprisoned in the dungeon with her, they can't see each other and are unable to talk. It is a somewhat strange comfort, however, just to know someone else is there. "Very bad food" is shoved under the door to her, and she describes her toilet as "a hole in the floor that stinks." She is always thirsty, her skin is dry, and her body is weak.

We explore her background and earlier aspirations for her life. She was taught to read and write as the daughter of the king, and she developed a passion for writing. Even in the dungeon, and with no hands, she dreams of writing a book. "The story is in my head," she says. "A woman who lives in the forest—she has a horse and travels freely. She goes to different places, has adventures." Our young writer feels that her original purpose was to have a home and belong somewhere. She dreams of living with her cousin and writing under an assumed name. "A male name: Federico!" she proclaims.

The young woman dies in the dungeon after an undetermined amount of time. She is relieved to die and happy to finally escape the horror and disappointment of this lifetime.

As we look at the lessons from this life experience, Carrie identifies that what she learned—"Don't speak! Don't write!"—was not the original intention for that lifetime. She points out that it could have been possible to live happily with the cousin and write under a male pen name, but she was careless and brought ruin upon herself. She misjudged her level of safety and left her writing lying around, so that it was discovered. She does realize that writing was a very key part of her expression in that lifetime, and it was shut down due to the times and circumstances.

In accessing her higher guidance, Carrie is encouraged to go ahead with her academic papers: writing is also important to her in the here and now. But she is also encouraged to sing and be in theater. Her guidance reassures Carrie that she has courage and strength that are drawn from many lifetimes, that she has been very courageous in battle in the past, and that she needs to prepare herself for future "battles" through prayer, spiritual work, and writing. This latter seems a bit out of context to me, but I trust that the purpose of the message will reveal itself over time.

A few months later, Carrie checked in with me by e-mail:

> Within the last three months my life has done a complete 180. I mean, it has really changed . . . I have definitely stopped feeling like I have been going crazy though. With the life I examined, it was very hard. One night I woke up and found that I was worried about my hands still being there or not. I have had some life changes related to the experience . . . Ironically I was fired from my job because I outed [myself] as a queer person . . . It was very strange; I guess their minds were stuck in the medieval times like my past life. There are groups all over the nation who have written letters for me to protest. I still have had some extreme difficulties in writing my own letter of grievance . . . [but then] totally unexpectedly I [was able to] speak in front of eighty people about my discomfort . . .
>
> I was doing better and then I was in a car accident and totaled my car and could not walk for three weeks . . . Then I was sick for another three weeks with a terrible cough . . . My neck is a wreck. I've had my tonsils out and still get strep throat . . . Lots of energy [gets] stuck in my throat. I am wondering if it is past life because I remembered a life of being hung. I would like to see if it is that or something else . . .

Well, it certainly appeared that Carrie's courage and strength had been called upon in the intervening few months. Since I knew very little about her from our initial session, the fact that she was lesbian now was news to me, even though the content of the first regression centered on that issue. Gender, as well as sexual orientation, is one of those things that we all seem to move around with from lifetime to lifetime. Nonetheless, it does appear that some individuals have a preference or proclivity to choose a certain gender more often. As it turns out, it really is unimportant whether I have details like sexual orientation, or many other aspects of a client's current life, when working with someone. Those issues that need to come forward will do so.

The fact that Carrie "came out" at work shortly beforehand very likely was what stimulated the sudden anxiety about writing her academic papers. If we do some digging, it is not uncommon for us to discover an activating event like this that restimulates the trauma from the prior lifetime, be it a similar occurrence, hitting the same age, or a personal encounter. I was interested to see what story would emerge in our next session focused on the throat and neck trauma. When Carrie returned to my office not long after, she expressed the desire to feel free to be herself even in the face of discrimination or oppression. We framed her question for the regression as: "What lifetime experience shut me down as far as speaking my truth?"

———

This time Carrie finds herself in pointy, flat shoes with laces and off-white linen pants. A white long-sleeved, pleated shirt with collar completes the outfit. She is a black man with very dark skin, short hair, strong and healthy, about thirty years old. There is an impression of dirt, sky, and dust, and wooden storefronts in a big town in the South [United States].

"I don't like it," he says. Then, with pride: "I just got blue shoes; they're handmade." The jump is a bit perplexing, so we explore his life in general to get a larger context for what is to come.

Things seem to be going okay in his life. He farms sheep; there's a corral with the animals. "I hear them," he says. He lives in a wooden house painted white, with a porch. It is one story and has a parlor and bedroom but no bathroom. "We have an outhouse," he explains. There are bright colors in the kitchen, and that's where we find his wife, Manny Rae.

He describes "a nice family life, happy and peaceful with my wife." [Manny Rae is later identified as Carrie's father in her current lifetime, and she does describe their relationship as "peaceful" as well.] There are three "young'uns": two boys, six and seven, and an older girl, about eleven. He identifies the year as 1866.

I direct him to jump to a significant event. He's won a contest; the prize is the blue shoes. He is very pleased with them.

We jump forward to the next significant event and find ourselves in the midst of a horrifying raid by the KKK (Ku Klux Klan). "They come to my house; they rape my wife; they tie me up!" I direct him to backtrack to the event that set off this terrible turn of fate. "I refused something . . . It was at a store . . . I wouldn't look at someone there . . . I just said, 'No, thank you,' and walked out. They said I had an attitude. I think it was jealousy over my success," he reasons.

Awful as it is, we return to the scene with the KKK to observe what happens in more detail. "My wife, she's barely alive. They raped her, popped [out] one of her eyes even, and forced me to watch! Their hatred is so disgusting. I would like to kill them, but I'm powerless; they've tied me up. The men hide themselves [under the white sheets] out of their shame and pride, but I know some of their eyes and voices."

He describes a horrible scene of torture and mayhem. "They have tied my hands and force a white gag in my mouth. They hit me with hammers, break my legs. They shoot me. They burn me. Finally they hang me. By then I'm unconscious. Why do they do this? We were living in peace, not causing any trouble! They're sick; there's no way you could say anything they'd listen to."

As we move through the death, look at the significance of that lifetime, and confer with higher guidance, Carrie suddenly comes out of her hypnotic state. The events of this regression were so horrific, I was amazed she stayed with it as long as she did. However, we did get some interesting reflections prior to her spontaneous termination of the session. It had been a good life until that unexpected event, full of friends, family, and neighbors. An interesting conclusion drawn from this experience, which addressed Carrie's desire to speak her truth, was: "Even if you keep your head down and don't speak, they still get you. So you might as well speak; you'll feel better."

The prior life's experience fueled a desire in the current lifetime to fix society, to right the wrong that was done. However, Carrie was advised by spiritual guidance that "the issue is too big; you can't solve it yourself. People have been fighting for centuries; there's too much to change." And instead she was counseled to work with the resulting anger. "Take time to acknowledge it, process and talk it through, and then release it." She was reminded that "there is no perfect place or community; we are here to learn our lessons." At that point Carrie jumped out of the trance she had been in.

———

Once again, Carrie and I corresponded by e-mail some time after her session. She reported that she was doing quite well now and wanted to share some interesting research she had done that fleshed out some of the occurrences in her last session:

> I am glad that I went back to do the second session. I am very fascinated with past lives now and feel that learning about past lives has changed the way that I see life very profoundly . . . I looked up that date [given in the regression] . . . It was the date that the KKK first got together after the ending of slavery.* I also learned that slaves weren't allowed to wear shoes because it kept them "like children" and the difference between a free black man and a slave was that the free person wore shoes.

---

* Historical data records the first Klan meeting as December 24, 1865. It would appear that the client's research was approximating the date, but it is within just a few days of 1866.

Shoes were very symbolic during the era of emancipation from slavery. My past life I won a pair of shoes, blue shoes in a contest and was very proud. The shoes meant that I was a free man and when I wore them they threatened the KKK people.

Carrie seemed to be one of those souls who are in what I like to call "spiritual postgraduate work." She signed up for lifetimes of great challenge, first being a gay woman in the late Middle Ages in a position of high visibility in a predominantly Catholic country. Then she had a lifetime as a free black man in the American South right after emancipation of the slaves. Although quietly pursuing her own life in each case, just being who she was threatened the belief systems of those around her, with dire consequences. In her current life as a gay Latina, she was continuing the theme of swimming upstream and learning to hold her own in the face of censure. Fortunately, in this life, this only meant losing a job rather than being tortured and losing her life. And in her current life, she experienced what it was like to have many people supporting and defending her. In integrating all of these experiences, she was finding her own voice to speak up in her own defense.

These stories once again point to the needless human suffering caused by intolerance based on rigid thinking and the fear of what is different. I hope that courageous souls like Carrie can help us evolve to a greater understanding of our human commonality and connection with each other.

ESSENTIAL TRUTHS UNCOVERED

* Taking care of one's personal safety balanced with speaking one's truth.
* Working to right society's wrongs while realizing that you can't solve them all yourself.

* Understanding that we are here to learn lessons and there is no perfect place or community.
* Acknowledging the suffering caused by intolerance.

EXPANDING YOUR PERSPECTIVE

The last two case studies have dramatically demonstrated the diversity of experience we find when we explore our prior lifetimes. In the previous chapter, Deanne, a professional Caucasian woman, finds herself to have been a man in a primitive village, then a well-to-do black man in the 1940s, and then a male teacher in India. In this chapter, Carrie, a gay Latina, finds herself to have been an imprisoned woman in medieval Spain and then a free black man in the American South. In each case, we find lifetimes and situations of extreme intolerance and in fact terrible violence committed against those who are considered different.

Truly seeing ourselves in another's shoes is one of the great gifts of past life work. How would your attitudes and opinions be impacted if these had been your regression experiences? Challenge yourself with this exercise: Think of the kind of person or group of people that you have the most difficulty relating to; perhaps there's a difference in religion, politics, race, or sexual orientation. Then imagine finding yourself in a lifetime when you are a member of that particular group: their identity and beliefs are what you were raised to believe in; this is what is normal for you. Can you be honest enough to step into that life experience? Can you be courageous enough to stay with it and empathize with their point of view? This is not an easy assignment, but it is a valuable one that can help each of us learn to integrate a much wider worldview and consciousness.

CHAPTER 7

The Misfit Monk

GEORGE WAS A successful businessman in his mid-forties. I was a little surprised by the nature of his request when he contacted me. He said that he had been raised Catholic but no longer practiced that religion. He considered himself spiritual, not Catholic. He wanted to use past life regression to explore the origins of what he described as his "unsettled feelings about organized religion, with its concern with power and rules, and its disconnect from love." Although many of the clients who come to see me are less than enamored by organized religion and more intent on forging their own spiritual paths, I never had someone ask to investigate why that was the case with a session.

George also mentioned that he frequently experienced a pain running down the right side of his neck, especially during times of stress. He wondered if we could find a past life origin of that as well. It frequently happens that, within the same lifetime, clients will find the answer to seemingly unrelated questions. I shared this with George, and he agreed that the religious question felt much more pressing to him and we should use that as our focus for the session. We could just see if the neck issue also came into play.

As George enters the regression, I have him bring his attention to his feet, and he notices buckled leather sandals. He is dressed as a monk, in a brown robe that hangs loosely, with a cord tied around his waist. He describes himself as having a round face and dark hair with a bowl cut to it, being rather overweight, and in his mid-forties to fifty years old.

He is standing on cobblestones and finds he is in a square or plaza in front of a church. He's a happy-go-lucky type of guy, out in the square, enjoying the good weather, looking around at the other buildings, and watching the horse carriages roll by. He is able to identify the time and place as 1776 in Florence, Italy.

As we move the scene forward, the monk enters the church. There's a large stained glass window with the sun streaming through it. He expresses awe at the beauty of the windows. Walking toward the back of the church, he begins to feel apprehensive as he nears a room at the back. He hears the voices and laughter of other monks who are in the room; feeling scared and disappointed, he stays away.

Some symbolic images seem to come up at this point in the regression. The monk sees a white sink with two drains, a black liquid flowing up from the drain and filling the sink. He also sees a man in a black robe and hood whose face is obscured. He questions whether this is himself or someone else, but he cannot connect with that information. He sees the figure presiding over a funeral and feels as if there has been an important shift for him related to this event, something he subsequently identifies as a loss of trust.

To get more solidly back into the lifetime, I direct the monk back in time to when he had joined the order. He is young, lighthearted, happy to be part of this religious community. But as we move forward again, a darkness begins to come over him. He is surprised and disappointed. "It's a different deal than I thought," the monk explains. "I thought it would be pure and holy, and we would treat others with love and respect. Instead it's a sham, like a fraternity to hang out in." He continues to have a sense of foreboding but can't figure out exactly what it's about.

I ask what impact this realization has for him. "I feel like an outsider—not one of the brothers," he says. "It's uncomfortable, doesn't feel right; there's bad energy," he says with dismay. He feels alone within his religious community with these feelings but continues to go about his daily activities, mostly keeping to himself.

I direct him to the last day of that lifetime. "It's that very day!" he exclaims, and then he begins to weep. "They [the other monks] chase me, throw me, and I fall down the stairs. I break my neck! I landed on my right side, and I'm lying there on the cobblestones, seeing the horses go by." He realizes that the other monks were trying to scare him and get him to leave because his piety made them uncomfortable and he didn't fit in. Things got out of hand, and his breaking his neck was an unintended accident. However, once this occurs, the other monks very callously hurry back into the church and close the door. He dies there on the cobblestones, alone and without any physical or moral support from anyone. Again he sheds a copious amount of tears full of grief and disappointment.

"I can't believe it! It's a beautiful, clear-blue day; the chapel is in front of me. Is this what this stands for? What this is?" he asks. He realizes that the funeral he saw earlier was his own. The feelings of loss of trust become clear.

Much value comes from processing this lifetime. It did indeed turn out that the single lifetime addressed the two seemingly unrelated issues that George first mentioned: his discomfort with organized religion, and the pain that ran down the right side of his neck. Rather than lessons learned, George is able to identify a number of questions that still linger from that life experience: "The confusion about church and conflict—does this have anything to do with God or spirit? Did God abandon me? Why did he leave me to die on the street in front of the church? Blind faith in God and goodness—was that a mistake? Beautiful windows but callous monks—is it all a show?" On the positive side, he does acknowledge that he stuck to his own truth, his own convictions in that lifetime, despite the high price he paid.

George sees important reflections of the monk's experience in his current life as he continues to seek answers about spirituality: "I still struggle but don't ask for God's help. I question if he's really there for me."

At the end of the session, George's higher guidance chimes in with calming reassurance: "Sometimes the life experiences don't make sense from where we stand. Have compassion for the situation; human life is not perfect. You tried your best. Trust in God, not in a church. Jesus loves you, he's real, he's God. Trust in God. Just let go of the pain of the past. Forgive yourself; forgive those who were a part of it; forgive God for the disappointment. Let go of trying to figure it out."

George returned to see me for another regression session a little over a year later. He had done some amazing spiritual work with a faith healer in the interim. George was still curious to see more specific details of the monk's lifetime or whatever else might be related to that. This time we got a mélange of various lifetimes—as a monk, a priest, a follower of Jesus—but none in great detail. In one case he identified with being a soldier who was chasing early Christians, and he surmised that it was important to see the balance of having been on either side of that dynamic. Another important image was of a priest who felt deep meaning and purpose in his work. He wished to share his vision, extend it to others—help move people away from their focus on the superficialities of daily life and move their attention back to the spiritual life.

The final scene in this second regression was a return to the death of the monk in Florence from the former session. It's the funeral scene again, but this time he feels less traumatized. He floats about the church feeling more at peace. "It doesn't matter how I died," he explained. "It's just a body." The key lessons George garners from this session are these: Keep following your gut instinct and your principles; you will be at peace with who you are. Apply the former personality's principles to your current life. Keep going on your path. That prior lifetime is in peace.

In discussion after the session, George felt that these final messages confirmed the shift he had sensed after his work with the faith healer. He now experienced a readiness to move forward minus the burden of his past life disappointment in God, the Church, and the spiritual life. He had integrated the experiences from his prior lifetimes in a way that would allow him to more fully explore his spiritual leanings.

ESSENTIAL TRUTHS UNCOVERED

* Accepting that human life is not perfect and requires compassion for situations we face.
* Letting go of the need to figure it all out, focusing on forgiveness instead.
* Following your principles, with trust that your intuition will lead to peace with who you are.

EXPANDING YOUR PERSPECTIVE

The number of people who identify themselves as "spiritual but not religious" continues to grow. How do you feel about your religious upbringing, if you have any feelings about it at all? Is there a religious or spiritual tradition you follow that enhances your life? If not, do you wish you had a religious community in which you found comfort and support? Or maybe you've left a traditional religion and are seeking a new spiritual path and community...

If you'd like to develop a more direct connection to your own sense of inner spiritual or higher guidance, you can take yourself through a similar process that I use with clients. Find a time when you can sit in a relaxing space and not be interrupted. Use whatever process works for you to focus your attention inward, be it following your breath, repeating a mantra or word, saying a prayer, or focusing on the sense of being surrounded by beauty. Then imagine a bright light in front of you that emanates a wonderful feeling of deep peace, joy, and divine love. Out of this light, a being comes toward you, one that is very wise, that knows and accepts everything about you, and that loves you unconditionally. Let yourself rest in the presence of this wise and loving being. After a while, ask this being what information or advice it wants to share with you. Trust whatever comes up—it could be in words, in pictures, or in a feeling. Ask for more explanation if it doesn't make sense at first. See if there's a gift that this being wants to give you.

Play with this exercise over a number of days and see what kind of connection you are able to establish with your inner guidance. Over time, the relationship can continue to grow and has the potential to become a rich resource you can call upon.

CHAPTER 8

Past Life Influences on Our Emotional Lives

ONE OF THE MAIN reasons people seek the help of a therapist is that they are struggling with some kind of emotional distress: depression, anxiety, feelings of guilt, or low self-esteem. Often clients will work for years in conventional therapy, come to a lot of intellectual understanding about their situations, and perhaps see the precursors in their current lives that seem to explain the dynamic. But they still are unable to make that leap into releasing the emotional patterns. These people are often feeling quite desperate that all the work they have done hasn't helped as much as they had wished, and they end up turning to alternative methods of healing, such as past life regression. Then there are those clients who really can't explain enduring feelings they have carried much of their lives that can't be linked to anything that has happened in their current lifetimes. Both categories are good candidates for past life therapy. Even more than physical symptoms, I believe we carry forward the unfinished emotional business, the belief systems and decisions about life and ourselves, from prior lifetimes into our current lives.

Here is a sampling of the types of emotional issues I have run into over the years, which have linked back in interesting ways to past life experiences.

Depression, Negativity, Grief

So many people today suffer from depression and negative feelings. As I mentioned in Chapter 1, it is important to make sure that the problem is not biochemical or events from the current lifetime. But even if there is some dynamic in the current life that could explain the depression, it can often also be linked to past life events.

We tend to find ourselves repeating situations that will enable us to work through unresolved issues or feelings. One client came in describing her experience of life as "living in a cloud of grief," although she had no reason that she was aware of to feel that way. We uncovered a lifetime as an Ohio farm boy who had to leave home and everything he loved to fight in a war overseas. His beloved grandmother died while he was away. Even though he survived the war and returned home, he was never able to reengage with life and died still carrying intense sadness and grief.

Another woman wanted to get to the source of her general feelings of negativity with which she approached life. We went to a life in which she was a mail-order bride. She received no love or sense of value from her spouse, and she felt very negative about her existence. However, she continued to choose security over self-expression to the day of her death.

In another case, a man who had battled with depression for most of his life that was not responsive to treatment, found himself as a Nazi soldier in World War II. He died in the war, feeling guilty and that he was a failure—realizing that not only had he not accomplished his patriotic mission, he was also leaving his family behind without resources.

Deserving Punishment, Self-hatred, Self-criticism

Some clients take the depression and negativity a step further and are battling with self-incriminating feelings. One client described his feelings toward himself as if he deserved to be punished, a feeling that did not connect with his current life. He went back in regression to ancient Rome. He was a soldier who actually defied orders on what he considered to be moral grounds. As a result, he was imprisoned and his family renounced him for the shame of his insubordination.

Similarly, a man who carried an unanchored sense of guilt and acknowledged that he was quite hard on himself went to a lifetime as a peasant who stood up to the tyranny of the ruling class. In times like those, it was not a judicious move, but he gave no forethought to the disastrous impact his actions would have on his family—for which he later felt intense guilt.

A woman who constantly battled feelings of self-hatred went to an experience as a male guard at Auschwitz who raped and killed a young female prisoner. He died feeling horrified at himself for what he had done.

Social Anxiety

Fear of other people, especially in groups, is a common anxiety that many individuals face. In my experience, serious social anxiety typically links to a dramatic episode of social humiliation (often re-sulting in death) in a prior lifetime. A young woman who was very uncomfortable in public situations to the extent that it impacted her work performance discovered a lifetime as a native African man who was captured, shipped to America, and sold on the block in the slave market. He was a tribal leader in his prime, but he became disgraced and degraded in public as he was poked, prodded, and treated like a piece of livestock.

A professional man who suffered a fear of really being noticed or "known" found himself in ancient Rome. He was a citizen-soldier who injudiciously insulted the government. He was arrested, stripped naked, put in chains, and died on display in the public square.

Another client, who said she just generally feared people, went to a Celtic lifetime when she was burned at the stake for being a witch due to her healing abilities. It's not difficult to imagine how experiences like these could lead to social anxiety if they were carried over from the past, unresolved.

Overdoing, Underdoing, Lack of Action

Activity patterns seen in the current life can sometimes be traced to prior life experiences, either behavior patterns or conclusions drawn from adverse situations. A professional woman consulted me about her pattern of "overdoing to the point of collapse," as she described it. She went to a lifetime as a male slave who was helping build the pyramids in Egypt. His job was to carry huge stones on his back from the quarry to the pyramid site. His days were an endless cycle of work and pain, until his death from exhaustion.

Another client had a maddening habit of starting but not finishing things. She discovered a Native American lifetime in which she lost her husband, her two sons, and finally her own life to the invading white men. Her conclusion at death was that all effort was useless; nothing she did could have an impact.

Another female client also visited a Native American lifetime. An artistic creator of pottery, this Comanche woman saw her village burned because the white men, in her belief, were fearful of the "bad magic" they imagined they saw in her innovative designs. In her current lifetime, this client said she feared her own creativity and couldn't get going on creative projects.

One man described himself as being "stuck in neutral" with his life, with lots of ideas but not really feeling as if he accomplished much of anything. He visited an early Roman lifetime as a wealthy, educated woman. She spent her time studying philosophy and esoteric ideas, but she never really applied all her intellectual learning to anything practical.

Fear of the Dark, Being Alone, Sleeping Issues

People have come in with a variety of fears concerning nighttime and sleep, from being afraid of the dark to having to always sleep in a particular position. Sometimes the client is just curious why that is, but sometimes these situations can be particularly debilitating when they impact proper sleep. What we discover in prior life events is usually some kind of deadly attack that took place at night.

For example, one client who felt extremely fearful when she was alone at night went to a lifetime as a young African boy who was killed in a night raid by another tribe. Another woman who described herself as being "afraid of going to sleep at night" uncovered this twice over: a lifetime as a young Jewish girl who was also killed in an unexpected nighttime raid, and a lifetime as a soldier who, on night watch, was terrified every night that he would fall asleep and allow the enemy to sneak past and kill his comrades.

Another client came in wanting to know why he could sleep only if his back was securely against the wall. He went to a Native American lifetime in which he was involved in a love triangle. One night, his rival sneaked in while he was sleeping facing away from the doorway and killed him with a deadly tomahawk blow.

Fear of Losing Love, Avoiding Love

In addition to clients who consult me for particular relationship dynamics with specific people in their lives, which I will discuss later, clients come to me with more generic relationship issues. It's not hard to imagine that these kinds of fears come from major losses in prior lifetimes.

A good example is one woman who consulted me regarding what she considered a general fear of losing love, which prevented her from getting too attached to anyone. She discovered a male peasant lifetime in medieval France, where the local lord coveted this peasant's beautiful wife. The lord kidnapped the wife and had the man thrown into prison, and his children were left orphaned, resulting in the loss of his entire family and his life.

A different male client described himself as always keeping lovers at arm's length. He visited a lifetime in the 1600s in which he never emotionally recovered from the death of a beloved wife. In fact, he shut down to such an extent that he kept his only daughter, also grieving the loss of her mother, at a considerable distance, doubling his loss.

Another young woman client fought feelings of panic whenever she imagined the possibility of losing her boyfriend. We uncovered a lifetime in the late 1800s in New York where a woman's entire family died in a carriage accident. She committed suicide in her grief and loss.

—————

With emotional issues such as these, sometimes just seeing the origin can greatly free up energy that has been blocked. In so many cases, the emotional impact of events such as the death of a loved one, one's own violent death, or some misdeed that the client perpetrated himself/herself is never fully processed in the lifetime in which it occurred. The individual dies with a lot of unfinished emotion, be it sadness, grief, guilt, anger, or any other difficult feelings. Typically, I will do emotional clearing work with the client at the end of a session to allow stuck feelings to be expressed, to move the individual toward completion and acceptance. We put the trauma in the past where it belongs, and we work to free the individual from its influence in his/her current life. At the same time we identify and integrate lessons of value that may be carried forward from the experience.

However, many emotional issues have also become habits of behavior and thinking in the current life. These habits need to be reworked in order to fully release the influence of the past life trauma that has been reinforced by habitual patterns in the current life. It requires awareness and dedication from the client to move forward in his/her life with new attitudes and behavior, which is something I work to instill in the session.

It's always intriguing to me to see the life stories that come up when people explore the source of current life emotional issues. Even though I can make a good guess at what type of trauma we are looking at, I never know what the life situation, the setting, or the details of the story are going to be. Client stories spread across time, cultures, races, genders, and political persuasions. The depth of feeling that comes up as clients reexperience the life events, especially when there is loss of significant loved ones, is quite moving. There are times when both the client and I have tears streaming down our faces as we walk through the events of the past.

Chapters 9 through 12 are detailed regression stories that demonstrate how deeply felt the emotional wounds of the past can still be if they have not been unearthed and worked through.

EXPANDING YOUR PERSPECTIVE

We all experience difficult emotions from time to time. In Jungian psychology, the personal quest for wholeness can be obtained only by incorporating both the dark and light sides of ourselves: anger and sadness are as important to embrace as joy and love. But when these dark emotions become entrenched or a habitual way of responding to events or people in our lives, it's time to regain balance.

Did any of the brief sketches above remind you of yourself or someone you know? What challenges do you face in your emotional life? This would be a good time to take out your journal and do a little exploring. Have you battled with anxiety, anger, guilt, depression, jealousy, or any other unpleasant emotion? Very often these emotions arise to protect us from something. For example, indecision may be protecting us from making a bad mistake; anger may be protecting us by encouraging us to react when we realize our rights are being violated. In what ways might your emotions be protecting you? Think about where this may have originated. Are there more productive ways that you could protect yourself from these unwanted events?

CHAPTER 9

Life Is Suffering

A LOCAL PSYCHOLOGIST who was familiar with my work referred Lori, a woman in her early fifties, to me. Despite quite a bit of work in conventional therapy with the psychologist, Lori reported that she experienced a feeling of terror and dread every day just after waking up. The past couple of years she had also been given a treatment known as BioSync, in which bilateral sound stimulation was used to reduce anxiety. Lori still experienced the feelings of dread. Although she held an office job, she explained that she lived a reclusive lifestyle and really only felt safe in her apartment, particularly in bed. As you can imagine, this was placing severe limits on her ability to live a full life.

I began to explore Lori's background to see if there were any events in her current life that might explain these feelings. She shared that the symptoms had begun at age seven when her father died suddenly from a heart attack. She described her mother as an emotionally abusive woman who did not allow Lori to grieve her father's death. She was essentially on her own with the sadness, confusion, and trauma. Lori explained that when just a first grader she felt responsible for her dad's dying, which can be a typical reaction in young children, who mistakenly believe that they actually cause many things that happen. She also believed it was her responsibility to prevent her mother from dying. A heavy load for a seven-year-old!

In addition, Lori shared that she was afraid of the ocean, and she was completely fascinated with World War II. She admitted a fear of being strangled, and she felt most safe being "in a small box, like a closet, that I can close and no one can find and hurt me." We entered the regression looking for the origin of the dread, feeling unsafe, and the desire to hide away in her house.

———

Lori's first impression is of bare feet, with dirt between her toes. This is usual and familiar to her. She is a girl, about eight or nine, and is wearing overalls with the cuffs folded around the knees and a thin shirt underneath. She has been running, playing in the sun with friends. Her dark hair is in pigtails. They are in the country, it's a pretty day, and she's happy playing with her friends. But then she notices a fearful, anxious feeling inside.

"Something's not right . . . I'm alone," she says. She sees a big house surrounded by trees, steps leading up to the door. But there is no one there.

Before moving further into what is obviously going to be a bad situation, I backtrack to learn about her family. She describes a man in black who appears to be in his fifties, with a tall black hat. "He's a super-Orthodox Jew with a tall hat and long beard," she explains. This is her father, and she reports feeling really safe and secure with him. "He's very strict, but he has a warm heart, a nice smile, kind eyes. Me, I'm the youngest—the only girl—and I'm the apple of my dad's eye." Upon inquiry, I discover that she believes she recognizes him as a former boss in Lori's current lifetime, with whom she had a very positive relationship.

She identifies three older brothers, envisioning them dressed both as farmers and in suits. They are all in their late teens, quite a bit older than she is. She feels safe with them also. "They spoil me," she remarks.

Her mother looks to be in her forties, wearing a plain dress with an apron. She's a little plump and wears her hair in a bun. She seems a little remote to the girl, and the girl states that she's closer to her dad. "I don't think she likes me," she comments. "She's critical a lot. I can't do anything right. She's not warm and affectionate like my friends' moms." She suspects that this is a stepmother and feels that they don't really belong to each other. Lori is able to recognize the stepmother as her first-grade teacher in this lifetime, a rather strict nun.

There also appear to be a couple of other adults in the family picture, and perhaps some cousins who are slightly older than she is. They don't appear to be significant figures.

We move to the activating event that caused the sense of anxiety. She is now about twelve. She is wearing a skirt and blouse, returning home from school, and no one is home. She searches and finds the house empty and cold. "What do I do? Where do I go?" she repeats, panicked. She doesn't trust the neighbors, because they've been un-friendly recently. "They ignore us, ostracize us," she says. She packs her things, feeling totally alone. "I should have been home! I could have prevented it! I should have been more careful!" she exclaims, unrealistically taking total responsibility for the situation.

"People ask me what I'm doing sitting on our steps with my suit-case," she says, "so I walk down the street toward town." I ask to see if we can identify the time and place she is in, and she immediately comes up with 1939 in Kraków, Poland. "There are crowds of peo-ple like me—families—and we've been told by the authorities to go somewhere." Men in uniforms herd them to the train station. She has the impression two men are looking specifically for her. "I try to lose myself in the crowd," she says. "I'm terrified, try to run, but I can't get through all the people."

The next scene is with a crowd of people in the country some-where, waiting. Her suitcase is gone. "People are being shot!" she exclaims, horrified. "There's a mass grave, and we're burying them! There's nothing I can do to help!" It appears she and other prisoners have been forced to perform this grisly task. She feels reassured that "at least I'm with my people; we're all together. I'm alone, but not alone." Unfortunately, this will not save her from the ongoing terror. The work detail, shoveling dirt over piles of bodies, is horrifying.

As we move forward, the girl finds herself off in the woods with a few other escapees. One is a school friend. "There were so many bodies . . . I feel guilty to be alive while the others are dead," she laments. "I don't deserve to live. How can people do things like this? We're all really depressed, sad, and lost. But we can't go back!"

The little band of six or seven escapees tries to forage despite not having much appetite after everything they have seen and been forced to do. They do the best they can for shelter, but they are essentially lost in the woods. One day the others go out to look for food but never come back. The girl is now entirely alone and without resources.

She begins to walk. She finds farmhouses where she steals food and finds safe, enclosed places to hide. "I can't be seen!" she insists. "I'm getting sick, but I keep walking. I've become very self-reliant, but I'm anxious. I can't relax for a second. I must be careful not to get caught. I am so alone!" My heart aches for this broken girl whose life has taken such a tragic turn.

Eventually she is found by troops; she's not sure if they are Russian or German. "I know it's the end," she says. She is stabbed in the solar plexus by a sword or bayonet and is buried while still alive. "I'm choking; I can't breathe," she panics. She is in total despair. *I don't want to die* is her last living thought. Then she feels enveloped by a bright light as she makes her transition, and she finally feels safe.

As we process this lifetime, Lori acknowledges that she was deeply wounded emotionally from this experience, and it hadn't been healed yet. Her higher guidance assures her that she is a good person, that she is loved, and that everything will be all right. Lori is able to identify some positives from that lifetime as well as acknowledge the horror. Some people were very kind, despite the circumstances, and being part of a family was an important and meaningful factor. She feels a resolve that the atrocity can never be allowed to happen again, and we cannot let people forget this. At the same time she exhibits an astounding level of compassion and understanding. "Everyone was a victim," she observes, "even the perpetrators. They didn't know what they were doing."

I give Lori some exercises to help cleanse the effects of that lifetime, a sort of daily maintenance routine with showers of golden light that can help clear the trauma on the emotional, physical, mental, and spiritual levels. We agree that she will return for more work, looking perhaps for an earlier lifetime that may have set up this experience.

_____

When Lori returned a month later for her next regression session, she reported that the morning dread had improved some and she was feeling more internal peace. However, leaving the house still felt threatening to her. She said her focus had shifted from the fascination with World War II and the Holocaust that she used to feel. She did three weeks of intensive research after the first regression session and then was done. That past lifetime now felt complete to her.

For this next session Lori wanted to work on an injury that she had sustained eight months earlier. She had developed acute tendinitis in her Achilles tendon, and it was not responding to physical therapy or orthotics. She had focused on her ankle with an energy worker and felt a deep sadness come up, as if there were "shackles around my ankles." She described the initial pain of the injury as if her ankle had been pierced. When clients come up with these kinds of "as if" descriptions of their symptoms, I use them as my entry point to the prior lifetime. "Go to the origin of the feeling of your ankle being pierced and being in shackles" was my directive.

_____

"There are shackles round my legs with a chain connecting them," Lori starts out. "I'm in a boat with oars. I'm seated at the oars." She is now in a man's body. His ankles are chafed and they really hurt. He is in an open boat, sitting on a bench with other men, also shackled. They are completely nude, and their bare feet are sitting in water as they man the oars.

I ask him to focus on his body. He describes himself as having a white complexion and a medium build. He feels very angry, trapped, and with no escape. He didn't know any of the other prisoners prior to being on the boat with them. "I'm a Christian imprisoned by Muslims," he says. "I hate them. I'm really afraid."

When I ask him to see how he got into this situation, he describes having been a crew member on a sailing ship that was attacked by the Muslims. He was taken prisoner and enslaved at the oars. "Even though I was a crew member," he reflects, "I was afraid of the ocean. I can't swim." (I know this to have been a fairly common situation from other client regressions to lifetimes as early seafarers.)

I direct him back to his earlier life to see the major events before becoming a crewman on that fateful ship. He identifies himself as English, and he sees himself running in the streets of London, alone and barefoot. He's anxious about survival and is afraid all the time. At age ten he's a loner, with no friends and no family. He has to forage for himself. When we go back even further, he realizes that his whole family died when he was six or seven, possibly from the plague, and he became a street urchin. He is not able to identify the year. This isn't surprising; it probably had no relevance for him at the time.

He goes on to describe his life on the street. He mostly tries to stay out of trouble and avoid people who might hurt him. There's lots of danger: gangs of kids who will bully or beat him up, and some adults who pose a similar danger. It's mainly other street people he has to watch out for. He hides to stay safe at night, but each morning when he wakes up it's back to the hunger, cold, and danger. He misses his family.

He first becomes a cabin boy on a sailing ship soon after. "I'm on deck, looking at the ocean. I don't swim; it's frightening. I constantly worry: *Is this the day I'm going to drown?*" As he becomes a young man, he is pressed into being a crew member. It's very hard work, and crewmen are punished if they try to escape. "I'm not quite as fearful of the ocean," he explains, "but I still don't like it."

The key turning point comes when "one of the crew up in the rigging catches sight of a corsair [a type of ship known to use slaves to man the oars starting in the 1200s]. We tried to outrun them, but they had oars, and we only had the wind." Most of the crew was killed or captured. "They had an iron dowel that they heated red-hot and were piercing the Achilles tendons of both legs, so you were crippled and couldn't run. Then they shackled us to the oars.

"I beg them, scream, 'Don't do it to me!' I'm asking for mercy, but there is none. I feel sick and scared: this is probably the end," he says, sounding completely hopeless. "It's survival of the fittest." His ankles ache constantly. He is angry and fearful, and there is no escape. Those who die are thrown overboard.

The corsair attacks another ship, and he is wounded. He is thrown overboard while still alive, but he can't swim. "I feel God has abandoned me. Why does it have to end this way? I hate God. I'm blaming God for the result of this life." He panics, drowning. As he breathes in the seawater, his final thought is: *Life is only hurt, pain, and suffering. All I want to be is safe in the next life.*

I immediately direct Lori to find the origin of this chain of pain and suffering. She enters another lifetime: there are stairs, a hallway, and doors leading off in different directions. The walls have "engravings like an Egyptian tomb," with animal motifs. "I'm afraid," Lori says. I suggest that we bring forth a guiding spirit that can accompany her on this exploration. It quickly appears in the form of a cat.

Lori is more comfortable now and able to proceed. The building is a temple with smooth white columns. It sits on a large hill covered in rich green grass and overlooking the ocean. It is a beautiful day, and she finds herself as a woman in the company of about five or six other women. They are all dressed similarly, in filmy, draped dresses, very comfortable. They appear to be temple priestesses.

"We've come out to enjoy the day and the view. It's so warm. The marble is a beautiful white against the green grass. I'm very happy," she says.

Suddenly, out of nowhere, a huge fiery boulder crashes through the columns of the temple. "My sister is very frightened; I try to comfort her. Then there's nothing."

She is able to view what has happened, however, from a higher perspective. "It's an explosion, a volcano: it's Pompeii," she says. She is likely referring to the famous eruption of Mount Vesuvius in AD 79. It destroys the temple, and she reports being unable to breathe. "I'm totally concerned for my sister; I want to protect her. I'm holding her, talking, reassuring, even though I know we're going to die. I need to be her strength so she doesn't panic at her death. I've always been courageous; she's been fearful. I'm a leader of this group. I'm responsible. But there's nothing I can do."

In this priestess's view, this is the judgment of the gods. "They are not pleased; people are turning away from the old ways. They aren't obeying the old laws; they're lazy. I fear the gods."

She begins to feel very sick and identifies a gas that seems to be covering them.

"I've done my best, but I've failed the gods. If I'd really done the job, this wouldn't have happened." She feels alone and abandoned by her gods. Her final thoughts are ones of despair: *It's all my fault! I should have tried harder . . . I'm being punished. I feel like I've angered the gods and don't deserve to live. They've abandoned me, but it's my fault . . . Death is the price. I was brought up all my life to serve the gods, but I've failed. It's right and proper.* She dies.

As we process these lifetimes, Lori identifies some beliefs she carried forward that have been far from helpful for her in her current life. Although she recognized that the street urchin/galley slave learned how to survive on his own, he learned that life is only pain and suffering. The legacy from that lifetime is the consuming desire to be safe. It related directly to Lori's morning fearfulness and obsession about being safe above all else in her current lifetime. The experiences of the Jewish girl caught in the Holocaust also directly relate to these issues. The galley slave's injury and trauma to his Achilles tendons and ankles was reflected in Lori's current problem with her Achilles tendinitis and pain.

Lori found some more beneficial lessons in the midst of the trauma and mistaken beliefs from the priestess lifetime. She loved her life and purpose of serving the gods. She had strength as a leader, had the respect of her other priestesses, and loved the sense of family they had built. Ultimately, though, she saw that she was unable to control the behavior of others. She equates her guilt and sense of being at fault about her father's death in this lifetime with the same feeling of responsibility for disaster and death in the priestess lifetime. A similar feeling of being abandoned by the gods/God, and the fact that she was being punished, has been carried forward into her current life.

When accessing guidance from the spiritual plane, Lori was told that "the feelings of morning dread, guilt, abandonment, sadness, depression—these all relate to the inability to protect your sister in Pompeii. It carries through to this lifetime. The only person you can be responsible for is yourself—not the world and not volcanoes. It is not your fault."

As we closed the session, I gave Lori some journaling work to do. Her guidance also indicated that there were other lifetimes that could be addressed at the appropriate time.

———

Two months later, Lori returned to continue clearing out the vestiges of past lifetimes. We directed our intention toward whatever was still anchoring the feelings of dread, sadness, and overwhelm that she experienced.

Lori identifies herself as a little girl of about five or six. She lives in the Black Forest of Germany, AD 900 to 1000, with her parents and her baby brother. As we enter the lifetime more fully, she feels warm fur boots on her feet, warm leggings, and a heavy long-sleeved tunic. "I feel nice and warm," she says. There's something heavy protecting her head as well.

She describes lots of trees. It's damp and dark. The sun doesn't penetrate, even during the day. We visit a scene where she is chasing a younger child through the trees, laughing and playing. They like each other, and she takes care of him.

I direct her to her home, and she describes a wood structure, dark, with a thatched roof, in the middle of the forest. There is snow all around. Then she comes to a group of dwellings, with people and horses and dogs. It's the nearby village. There are lots of men talking, and they greet her. "They know me; I know them," she says. She has come to town with some others on an errand but is now hanging out while the business is being handled. She's on her own in the village but feels safe and warm.

As we move forward, feelings of apprehension begin to build. It feels tight and empty in the area of her solar plexus. "Something's wrong," she says. "I'm afraid. I feel abandoned. Someone's died."

As the scene unfolds, she finds herself alone in the snow-covered forest. She feels total shock, loss, grief, and abandonment. "There's no one there for me. I don't know what to do! I'm shattered in a million pieces and can't put it back together." She begins to weep dramatically with pain and sadness. "I feel like I don't exist. It's blown up. There's nothing left. I feel like I've died too. I'm not alive. I can't cope. It's total overwhelm."

As a six-year-old child, she doesn't understand. Someone she really loved and depended upon, "someone who's always there for me," is gone. "People are trying to explain to me, but I don't get it," she says.

We step back from the intense emotions and begin to unravel the events that transpired. It appears that her father begins to drink heavily and, when drunk, beats her mother. Her mother, who sees this coming, sends the girl to hide in the forest with the baby.

One day she comes home from the forest and her mother isn't there. "I'm looking for her in the forest, but I can't find her!" It appears her father has finally killed her mother in one of his drunken rages.

I decide to set up a conversation between the girl and her mother, to help process the feelings and unfinished relationship between them.

"Why? I don't understand!" the girl cries.

"It happened," her mother replies. "One of the negative events of life, out of our control. I didn't want to go."

"I miss you! I want you back! It's so empty. I want to stop feeling . . . it hurts too much."

"I love you," says the mother. "It's okay to mourn."

"I don't want to continue living," the girl replies.

"You'll be fine," her mother assures her tenderly.

We identify the spirit of this mother as Lori's father in her current lifetime: the father whom she loved so much but who died when she was seven years old. The abusive father from the past lifetime is identified as her deceased father's first wife, with whom he had a violent relationship this time around as well. The baby brother appears to be her current mom, which also explains Lori's sense of responsibility for her mother's well-being in this lifetime.

Returning to the story, the girl helps bury her beloved mother and then takes her place doing the cooking and caring for the baby. Eventually her father strangles her to death in another drunken rage. "I really didn't want to keep living anyway," she claims. "And the neighbors foster the baby, so he will be fine."

As we process that lifetime, I want to clear the vestiges of unfinished business with that abusive father and ask her to bring him forward. "I feel apprehensive; I'm afraid of him," she says. "He used to hit me. I could never please him; I felt that everything was my fault. I never knew what mood he'd be in. My mother was my only protection." We bring forth a protective shield that surrounds her so he cannot do any harm. She says to him, "I don't want to talk to you," and then erases him from her mind. "I feel better; he's gone," she says. Sometimes clients' processes are surprisingly simple.

We proceed with the image of erasing the trauma from that lifetime. I instruct Lori to present all the images and feelings on a large whiteboard in her mind's eye. I figuratively give Lori a big eraser and have her wipe the board clean. Then I have her write all the positive feelings she wants to implant in her being: safe, secure, protected, free, happy, empowered, content, cherished, loved. All of these go onto her internal whiteboard to bring forward into her life now. I instruct her to repeat this practice for herself on a frequent basis.

In accessing Lori's spiritual guidance, she is told: "It's okay; you're doing fine. Everything is a choice on the spiritual level; there are no wrong choices. The lesson is in being strong and that it's natural to grieve. Great challenges on the human plane do not mean it was a wrong choice."

She also is given direction to clear out the remnants of her morning feelings of dread and being overwhelmed. "To release the morning feelings, the path is to tap into the feelings and cry. You can't do it alone at home. The work is to get relaxed and into the feelings enough to cry in the presence of another. This will relieve them."

Lori was well on her way. She had done a considerable amount of weeping in my presence. This lifetime may have had precursors, but it appeared to be the anchor of the worst of her fears. This was a case in which we had to do a considerable amount of digging over a number of sessions, but it proved to be very helpful for the client. Lori contacted me briefly sometime after the regressions, letting me know the effects had been lasting and conveying her gratitude for our work together. The potential for a whole new approach to life was opening up before her as she integrated the information from our work together.

ESSENTIAL TRUTHS UNCOVERED

* Extending kindness to others even in terrible circumstances.
* Taking responsibility for oneself only, not for others or for world events.

* Understanding that having great challenges does not necessarily mean we made the wrong choices in life.
* Rising above victim/perpetrator definitions to see that all parties to violence are victims.

EXPANDING YOUR PERSPECTIVE

Belief systems that have been carried forward can be powerful unconscious programming in our current lives. If you experienced the series of lifetimes that Lori recalled, what beliefs do you think you might have formed? Are there beliefs in your current life that are not serving you well, such as "I can't be vulnerable," or "I have to do it all myself," or "Love never lasts"?

Even if there are present life experiences that seem to reinforce these beliefs, is it possible that you've been experiencing what you project from unconscious expectations? What might happen if you were to release those beliefs that hold you back? When you take the first steps of releasing old wounds and beliefs, as Lori did, you may feel vulnerable and emotional as you grieve the loss of what used to be in order to transform into what you can be. As Lori's higher guidance reminded her, it's natural to grieve. You need to relax through the feelings and trust yourself. If you can find a trusted friend or counselor to sit with you as you allow yourself to freely express your sadness and grief, the healing will be that much quicker. It may feel very scary at first, but if you select your confidant carefully, most people are honored to support you in that way.

CHAPTER 10

I'll Lose Myself

KALINDA WAS IN her early forties when she first consulted with me. I found her to be an intense, intelligent, and very personable woman who was troubled about love relationships and her life's direction. She described herself as very independent and liked doing things on her own. She was raised in India in a very conservative-minded Indian family, and as she grew up she frequently clashed with her mother on this account. She felt she carried feelings of inadequacy from this failure to live up to her family's conventional expectations for her. When she was in her mid-twenties, her parents arranged a marriage with the son of family friends who was living in the United States. Kalinda saw a great opportunity to explore the U.S. and hoped she could fulfill her family's wishes for her future.

However, once in the States, Kalinda decided she could not go through with the marriage and broke the engagement despite her parents' protests. This caused quite a bit of tension within the family. Kalinda remained in the U.S., found employment, and established her independent life.

Kalinda actually described herself as having "relationship phobia," fearing that she would never be able to be herself in a committed relationship and that she would be dominated by her spouse. Of course, these fears were somewhat consistent with her family's modeling. She described her mother as insecure and "squashed by her husband and in-laws," and described her father as the one who made all the decisions. Still, Kalinda's fear was so strong that she believed that there was more to the story than her current life experience would account for.

About a year and a half before consulting me, Kalinda dove into what she considered a "major transformation," taking up regular meditation and yoga and returning to India for a long visit. Although she was involved in other therapy to address symptoms of depression, when she read some of Dr. Brian Weiss's books, she decided it was time to explore past life regression work. Our entry point was the past life that formed the root of her fear of a committed relationship and the sense that she would be dominated and unable to be herself.

———

The initial impression is of a cobblestone street, which Kalinda quickly identifies as being in Canterbury, England. It becomes clear that she is in a male body, wearing heavy metal armor and leggings with boots to the knee. A young man in his late teens, his brownish hair hangs straight to his shoulders. He describes himself as having "delicate features, a clear complexion, and fair skin."

He sees the tall spires of the cathedral in the twilight, but the street is empty. *Where is everyone?* he wonders. A feeling of heaviness and sadness overtakes him.

"It's war and destruction." He focuses in on a scene of fighting in an open field. "I'm fighting the Viking invasion; there's lots of killing," he observes. He feels very angry. "We must win and push back," he asserts. "The Vikings are hairy and mean!" With his comrades-in-arms, they successfully fight off the invaders, and he comes out of the battle without injury. There are fires in the streets of the city, however, and a lot of damage, and the people have fled.

I direct the young man to his home so we can get some context for this lifetime. He describes it as "a mansion, wealthy, upper-class, with many rules. It feels tight, rigid—we must maintain appearances."

Family meals are taken at a long table, with distance between the formally dressed diners. Servants wait nearby, watching impassively. He doesn't seem very at ease with the stiltedness at home and describes mixed feelings about his family. "I'm on the outside," he comments.

We move forward to see him being sent off to battle by his father. "It's to maintain the family name, the family honor," he points out. "My father is proud of me, not for me [who I am], but more for the image" being upheld. There is none of the typical fatherly advice about taking care or looking out for his personal welfare in the upcoming fighting.

As we move forward to the next significant event after the battle, the young man finds himself at a hillside graveyard. His father has died. "There's no real big emotion, just a little sadness," he says. The next important event finds him in a grand salon, attending a dance. He's watching the dancers, a little bored. Then a young woman catches his eye. She's smiling boldly, so he asks her to dance. He finds her charming, in her creamy gold dress and with her hair done up. "We don't talk much," he says, but some connection is established. Soon after, she becomes his wife.

They appear to have a warm relationship. "I feel very protective and tenderhearted," he says. "There's lots of contact; we hold hands and the like. I'm generally sad, but she lightens me," he observes. I probe to discover the source of his general sadness. It appears that his mother is quite ill: he sees himself sitting next to her, holding her hand, as she lies sick in bed and suffering.

However, a highlight in his life is his son. He sees himself and his son laughing and smiling, eyes sparkling, playing on the lawn. They splash in the fountain together. "I don't care about [damaging] the clothes!" he comments. He is trying to set a family culture that is different from the strict, impersonal one in which he was raised.

As we move to his death, he observes that he has had a long life that he's generally happy with. However, there is a feeling of loss and wasted time. "I wasn't able to show the depth of emotion and caring

I had," he regrets. "I couldn't say what I truly felt." He made strides in overcoming the family stoicism, but apparently not as much as he would have wished.

As sometimes happens with clients, Kalinda jumps immediately into another lifetime after this death scene.

She sees an angry face. "I'm a woman. I'm in a bedroom and a man is shaking me, yelling at me," she describes with fear in her voice. "I'm afraid, but I'm stubborn. I won't cry," she insists. He pushes her and she hits a big brass pot, which falls over.

Apparently this man, her husband, is routinely abusive. "I'm holding myself, shutting out the abuse," she says. The husband drinks and wastes all their money. She takes care of the house and has "no authority or decision making [power] about the money," she explains indignantly. She identifies the location as northern India.

The next scene is of a burning pyre. "I climb in!" she exclaims with horror. "My husband has died, so I'm supposed to join him in the pyre!" She wants desperately to escape this fate. "I hate him and I hate this tradition! I'm not afraid of the fire," she explains, but remarks again on the amount of hatred she has for her husband. "This isn't right! He was a mean, brutal man, and now I have to give my life for him?" She fights to avoid this terrible, untimely, and meaningless end to an unhappy life.

Other people force her into the pyre, and her dying thoughts are of vengeance. "This should change," she insists. "It's better to be alone than to live and die like this."

This case is a wonderful example of how, as a therapist, I must trust the client's process. Even though our original request was for the origin of Kalinda's relationship phobia, the first lifetime that came up appeared to be more of an affirmation of the value of relationships. Our Canterbury gentleman described himself as having a warm relationship with his wife, which included a lot of physical contact and tenderness. They had a long and overall happy life together and enjoyed raising their son. If anything, it was a lesson in connection and the honest sharing of feelings, and demonstrated the potential that there could be in a warm, loving, committed relationship. Even though he wasn't totally satisfied himself with his progress, the personality actually overcame much of his upbringing and was able to create a much warmer and personal family environment than the one in which he was raised. In processing this lifetime afterwards, Kalinda felt this was important for her to realize in her current life—that she, too, could overcome a strained upbringing and create a joyous connected family for herself. This was an important step toward integration.

I believe Kalinda's higher knowing guided her to see this vision of a positive marital relationship and affirm what is possible for her in this lifetime before exposing the memory of the terribly abusive relationship in India. Our psyches have self-protection mechanisms built in, and seeing the physical violence and death without having seen the more positive relationship might have only reinforced her fear of relationships. Having looked at the chain of events in the Indian lifetime, it was no wonder that Kalinda had carried forward the fear of being powerless and losing herself in a committed relationship. In that time and society, she was the helpless victim of her husband's abuse, with no rights and no voice. In fact, the ultimate "loss of self" came when she had to give up her own life because her hated husband had died.

I assisted Kalinda in a considerable amount of processing of that life experience after the regression and again in some follow-up counseling sessions. She mused that being back in the traditional Indian culture had undoubtedly reactivated issues from the abusive relationship. This is not at all unusual. We return to an area of the world, experience an event, or reach a similar age when something traumatic happened in a prior lifetime, and that reopens a Pandora's box, so to speak, for the issue to resurface and be addressed. I used guided imagery with Kalinda whereby she went back into the events of that prior Indian lifetime, stopped the abuse, destroyed the house where it happened, and walked away with the full support of her family. She was able to verbalize empowering statements such as "STOP! I'm human. How would you feel?" and "No one touches me this way again."

Further imagery work involved creating a quality relationship with a loving, supportive, protective male figure. As they joined hands, Kalinda was able to articulate what she wanted and deserved in a relationship: "I want honesty between us no matter what. Be there when I really need you. Let's laugh together, share, and enjoy each other." She saw herself feeling light, content, and playful, as she and this male figure watched a beautiful sunset on a lovely beach. A real sense of openness and possibility for the future was replacing the former relationship phobia.

ESSENTIAL TRUTHS UNCOVERED

* Sharing feelings honestly with the people in your life.
* Overcoming your upbringing to create the life you want.
* Stopping abusive relationships. It's better to break norms than accept abuse.

EXPANDING YOUR PERSPECTIVE

Articulating what we want and knowing on a deep level that we deserve it is a good start toward reaching our goals. How do we know we've gotten there if we've never identified the destination we seek? This can apply to relationships, career issues, health and wellness goals—whatever we'd like to accomplish in our current life. The next step is to believe and affirm that we already have what we seek, knowing that it just hasn't manifested itself yet. I suspect most of my readers are familiar with the use of affirmations: statements written in the present tense, using only positive language, that express goals as if they have already been achieved. For instance, you would work with the statement "I have financial abundance in my life now," not "I'm going to get out of debt someday soon."

Before we can successfully work with affirmations, however, many of us need to clear out the entrenched doubts and negative messages that may be holding us back. Many of these messages are unconscious and we only know they're there because we aren't getting the results we desire. One way to uncover them is to use your journal to set up a dialogue with yourself: At the top of the page, write your goal, and underneath it write all the reasons and excuses that pop into your mind why this isn't possible for you. Let this be a stream-of-consciousness exercise. The reasons don't even have to make sense. Just see what comes up. For example: that only works for other people, I'm being naïve, I'm asking too much, my friends would be jealous, I'm too fat, I'm too thin . . . The reasons may go on and on.

Then close your eyes and take a few deep-cleansing breaths as you allow yourself to drift to a beautiful, meditative space. Imagine there is a large whiteboard in front of you, and all those negative messages and limiting beliefs about yourself and the world are written on the board. Picture them cluttering up the whiteboard. Give yourself a large magic eraser, and imagine yourself wiping that board clean, so that all the clutter is gone. Now see yourself writing your new beliefs and affirmations on that whiteboard instead. Envision yourself having exactly what you want. Make this vision as real, as detailed, as you can. Allow yourself to intensely feel what it would be like.

This is an exercise you can repeat whenever you feel limiting thoughts intruding on your progress toward your goals. Once you have neutralized these limiting beliefs, you can move forward to envision and affirm your possibilities in many different areas.

CHAPTER 11

The Case of the Bad Traveler

RICHARD AND NATALIE, a professional couple, decided to come to see me and make a weekend of it. We planned an individual session for each of them, but there was a degree of uncertainty whether both sessions would happen or if the weekend would come off as planned at all. I found out more when I met them.

Natalie was providing the impetus behind the past life sessions, having read some of Dr. Brian Weiss's books and other metaphysical material. She not only wanted to have a session for herself, she also wanted Richard to have the experience. An easygoing fellow, he wanted to indulge her but had some mixed feelings about the whole thing, and on Friday afternoon he was still unsure whether he wanted to go through with his session that was planned for the next morning. I told him I would work with Natalie and then he could make up his mind after she reported back to him on her experience.

The issue Natalie wanted to address turned out to be another reason the sessions had been under question. She described herself as a "bad traveler" with extreme anxiety about leaving her home unattended, something she couldn't explain from current life events. She admitted this had even come into play around the regression weekend plans. Richard was quite hopeful that a session would resolve this for his wife as well, as it was putting a considerable damper on their ability to travel. So we sent Richard off while Natalie and I settled in for the next couple of hours to do our work.

————

After the usual relaxation process, I direct Natalie to go to the origin of her anxiety about leaving her home unattended and what might happen to it while she is away. Her first impressions are of an umbrella-like Chinese hat. She is a little girl about seven or eight years old, wearing clothes of a rough burlap-like material. She is riding in a cart drawn by an animal of some kind and sees mountaintops around her.

She looks out and sees a man close by with black hair and a mustache and dressed in similar clothes. He's riding on a horse or donkey and appears to be supervising a convoy of people through a mountain pass. There are both people and animals stretched out ahead of and behind the cart. The girl doesn't feel that this man is particularly significant to her; he's just what she's watching from the cart.

"It's scary! Why are we going?" she whines. The girl doesn't seem to grasp what is happening. I ask her if she is alone in the cart, and she realizes that there is a somewhat portly, mature woman riding with her. The girl describes the woman as "kind enough" and she does feel safer in the cart with the woman there. When I check to see if this figure is someone Natalie knows in her current life, she doesn't recognize her. In fact, later in the regression the girl says that this woman isn't a relative or anything; she's been assigned to take care of her but the girl doesn't particularly know her or like her all that much.

In order to learn more about what is taking place, I direct her to the beginning of the caravan's journey. She finds herself in a small gathering of reed huts in a temperate area of the mountains. She is playing with other children, running around after a meal. "It's fun and normal," she says. Then suddenly all the animals are being packed up, she is loaded in a cart, and they are heading for the mountain pass. The girl is quite disturbed that they seem to be permanently leaving their home. Eventually she comes to understand that war is involved and they must flee because an attack on the village is forthcoming.

When we attempt to identify location and era, she knows she is in China but can only identify the time as "primitive."

We return to the journey in the cart. The caravan is stuck in the mountain pass, because it becomes too narrow for many of the carts to negotiate. There is a steep gorge that drops off to the side and the little girl feels very agitated and afraid. "I'm stuck in this cart and I want to get out, but the woman won't let me," she complains. However, they somehow make it through and arrive at a clearing where the caravan breaks for a rest.

Children are running around again, as children do, and the little girl isn't as afraid anymore, although she's not happy. "Everyone is here, but it's not home," she insists.

When I instruct her to move forward to the next significant event, she moves into a situation she describes as all cloudy, as if something is trying to get in the way. "It's smoke," she realizes. "I'm under the smoke; it's above me. I'm in a big room, on the floor looking up at the smoke, and I can't get up. I'm watching with no feeling; it's weird."

Natalie realizes that she is a different girl now from the Chinese girl who lost her home. (Natalie has spontaneously moved into another prior lifetime.) As the smoke clears, she recognizes the room as a familiar bedroom where she sleeps, upstairs in an old two-story house in the country. There is a barn and trees in the yard and what looks like a lot of dry grass in the fields, which she guesses may be wheat. She sees herself as a nine-year-old girl wearing a brown dress patterned with little flowers.

I direct her to the last family meal, and she comments that she likes being around the wooden table with everyone. We meet two younger siblings, a boy and a girl, and a loving mother with blond hair wearing a gray dress. Her father appears to be her primary focus. He wears a hat and overalls and she says he's a farmer. He's typically a happy man, although he's upset about something at the moment. "But we're all happy," she says. She identifies the mother as one of Natalie's friends and her father as reminiscent of Natalie's father in her current life.

We jump forward to an important event, and the girl finds herself outdoors. It's hot and clammy and she's under a tree watching the wind in the dry grass. The wind picks up dramatically. There's a loud noise and she realizes something, perhaps a board from the roof, has fallen. "Someone's underneath it!" she exclaims. "It's my little sister. She's hurt badly. She's not moving and I can only see her feet." She is extremely upset. "Somehow it's my fault! I'm the big sister and I was supposed to watch her!" She tries but can't lift the heavy board, and no one else is home.

"I didn't mean it!" she wails. "I wasn't paying attention. What am I going to do?" She feels as if she were paralyzed and can't think. There are no neighbors nearby to help and her parents have gone somewhere. There is no way to reach them.

When I probe deeper to determine why she feels so responsible for this accident that occurred in the windstorm, she explains, "The wind blew it over, but I should have had my eye on her. Maybe if she was standing with me she would have been safe."

When her parents return home to this tragedy, she has remained next to her little sister, who is lying dead beneath the board. She is still numb with shock, grief, and guilt. A week later, at the wake for the dead child, she is alone in the parlor. "I feel ashamed of myself; I didn't protect her," she says. "I feel outside the family and lost without her. I am so very sad."

We attempt to determine whether this little sister is once again with Natalie as a figure in her current life, but she seems to be too blocked with guilt to focus on who this individual might be.

I direct her to jump forward five years. She's now about fourteen and still feels very much alone. Her mother seems to have aged from the experience, and her father now appears generally sad. "We lost our happy household," she observes dejectedly. "My parents love me; they're not angry," she says, but she still feels the accident was her fault. She notices that her little brother, who is now about seven or eight years old, doesn't talk much.

In another five years, not much has changed. She is still at home and still very sad about her sister. "There's an event—the anniversary of my sister's death. I'm so upset I can barely breathe." She feels trapped with the grief, guilt, and sadness. "I want to leave but I feel stuck. It's time to go. It feels like an anchor choking me. If I could get away, I could move on."

And indeed, when we move forward to the next important event, she is leaving home with sadness but also relief. She settles in a small town where she finds work in a restaurant. All of this is new to her, so it takes quite a bit of resolve. "I walked in and looked around; I'd never been in a place like this!" she proclaims. She identifies the year as 1928 but can only name the location as "the mountains."

I move her to the last day of that lifetime. She has long white hair and is over seventy years old. "I'm bitter, still upset about my sister, and feel very alone," she comments. I ask about a family of her own, and she shares that she eventually had a couple of children herself. She doesn't feel them around her and is upset that they aren't there. She recalls her husband as a tall, quiet man with brown hair. "I loved him; we had a good marriage, but I never felt I deserved it. He died and I miss him," she adds.

"I don't want to die bitter," she continues. "I'm saying to myself, *Why are you dying bitter?* It's bitterness for bitterness's sake. I wasn't really happy my entire life. I felt very alone." This seems to contradict her comments about love and a good marriage, but the fact that she never felt she deserved it must have kept that sense of aloneness and isolation in place and prevented her from forming close bonds with her children.

As we look at the key lessons from this second lifetime in particular, the number one observation is "I should have forgiven myself; I missed so much of life due to grief and sadness." Another important lesson emerges about staying connected to deeper feelings and not becoming hardened on the inside. The value of time spent with children is noted. Then, to our surprise, the image of doing laundry pops into her mind. Natalie interprets this as referring to the need to wash things clean. Briefly, the Chinese lifetime is labeled as a child's anxiety about leaving home, which she can now release.

Natalie's aunt appears as a wise and loving guide at the end of her session. The aunt has quite a bit to say about Natalie moving forward with her professional activities, to find her "next big thing." She also tells Natalie that it's okay to let herself have a happy marriage this time. The aunt offers Natalie the gift of a wonderful image of turning her inability to forgive herself from both past and current lives into stardust and having the stardust twinkle away.

For homework, I ask Natalie to continue to use that stardust image while she uses tapping (EFT, or emotional freedom technique, something she told me she was familiar with) to release her remaining sense of guilt. I also suggest she communicate regularly with the personality of the young Chinese girl to reassure her that she's safe in the world, whether or not she is in her original home.

————

The two lifetimes that came up related to Natalie's anxiety about leaving her home unattended from two different perspectives. In the first, we reexperienced a child's anxiety about the loss of her home and sense of security. As far as we know, nothing terrible happened to her other than the fact that she had to leave her familiar surroundings and she was scared and confused. Some of these childlike reactions seem to have carried forward into Natalie's current life.

The second story of the young girl who blamed herself for her little sister's death was heartbreaking. It demonstrated what tragedies can indeed happen when a responsible adult is not keeping an eye on the home front. Of course it's very possible that the same accident would have occurred even if the parents had been home, but the older sister probably would not have carried the same sense of responsibility and guilt if they had been there. These events seem to have crystallized in Natalie's psyche as a deep anxiety about leaving her home unattended. Experiencing a neighbor's home fire and a burglary in her current life may have been just enough to activate this past life trauma.

I checked with Natalie a few weeks after the session and she reported, "There has definitely been a shift in our personal and interpersonal energies . . . all for the positive. Probably the prevailing feeling has been one of peace. Life takes on a whole new meaning when you look at it as your soul's journey." She was looking forward to challenging herself with an upcoming trip across the country in the near future.

In the meantime, we'll have some fun with her husband Richard's experience in the next chapter.

ESSENTIAL TRUTHS UNCOVERED

* Forgiving yourself; wash clean your grief and sadness or you will miss what life still has to offer you.
* Staying connected to your feelings; don't become hard on the inside despite life's challenges.
* Valuing precious time spent with children.

EXPANDING YOUR PERSPECTIVE

Forgiveness is such a huge topic and so many books and spiritual practices have been devoted to that subject alone. Nonetheless, here is an opportunity for you to look again at what areas in your life are asking for a compassionate and forgiving heart. You may need to forgive yourself, you may need to forgive others—or maybe it's God or the slings and arrows of life's outrageous fortune. Use your journal to explore the ways in which holding on to "unforgiveness" may be causing you to miss out. Can you fully engage your own life if you are holding on to that unforgiving attitude? What does it do for you to hang on to it? Is it worth it?

CHAPTER 12

A Birthmark as a Bonus

WE MET RICHARD and Natalie in the preceding chapter. After Natalie's very successful session, Richard decided that he would indeed go ahead with a regression of his own the following morning. He had not done any reading about past life work, nor did he practice any meditation, yoga, or relaxation disciplines. When I asked him what he'd like to investigate, Richard figured he ought to ask about an unusual birthmark he had on his chest, because Natalie was convinced it was from a prior lifetime and she was dying to know all about it.

I probed a bit to see if there was something else that might be a priority for Richard himself. He mentioned his childhood. He had been so upset when his father left after his parents' divorce that he developed medical problems. Although he didn't see much of his dad after that, he always felt extremely close to him and his father's recent death had impacted him deeply. So we decided to toss out Natalie's agenda and focus on Richard's relationship with his father instead, asking for a lifetime that would explain the closeness between the two of them.

Richard described the feeling he's had since childhood related to the loss of his father as "like my stomach is being torn out." He believed they knew each other in a unique way despite not having much time together. So I asked him to focus on those feelings as he allowed himself to be drawn into a lifetime that would explain the loving connection between them.

Lastly, I advised Richard that many times we find that the various issues we consider investigating end up being related, so even though we would ignore the birthmark question, it was always possible it might show up on its own. Perhaps we could satisfy Natalie's curiosity as well.

———

He finds himself as a clean-cut young man in his mid- to late twenties, in a neatly pressed military uniform from another era. He's laughing with a comrade-in-arms with whom he's served in the military for a good while. They became close friends very quickly in the life-and-death situations they have faced fighting together. We quickly identify this man as Richard's father in his current life.

In the next scene, the two men are traveling in a military boat along with other soldiers. He realizes his friend, although of similar age, has a higher rank than he does and is the officer commanding the boat. As the commander, his friend has knowledge of what they will be facing up ahead, but he hasn't shared it with the rest of the men yet. Our soldier suspects nervously that they're headed to a battle somewhere, having set out from Italy on this boat. Sure enough, as they approach their destination the officer reveals that they are approaching a nasty, well-nigh impossible battle and they must be prepared to fight to the death.

The boat is approaching a beautiful beach in Croatia. (Richard's current personality emerges with the recognition of the exact beach from the travels he's done in Croatia.)

"Hey, Dad, it's too quiet," he says to his friend and officer. "What's up?" Ironically, it appears that the entire fighting unit has given their commanding officer the nickname "Dad" because he looks out for them all. They realize that on the higher ground in the brush, there's an ambush waiting for them.

"Why go that way?" he argues with Dad. "It's not good."

"That's the way we've been ordered to go," his friend answers with resignation.

It's not the right way, he thinks. *It's not the right way!*

Before he knows it, Dad is running up the beach and is shot. It's instantly fatal; Dad is gone just like that. *It should have been me,* he rails at himself. *I'm not as important. Why? He didn't have to lead the charge like that. He's always so passive usually. Why did he do that?*

Our soldier takes command and leads the other men onto the beach. Dad's body is floating in the shallow water, and the young soldier is determined to pull it up on the beach despite the shooting around him. Suddenly and very unexpectedly, the opposing forces come out of the bushes and make overtures of peace. "Let's go have a glass of wine," they offer. It makes no sense at all to the men who have just seen their beloved commanding officer cut down.

But they all go into a little village and have a drink together. It appears that Dad's death has calmed everyone down. Everyone looked up to him, including the Croatians. He was a prominent, well-loved figure and his death shocked some sense into them all. Our soldier negotiates a deal that settles the conflict, arranges a hero's burial for Dad, and then goes on to become governor of this war-torn area.

In the next scene, he's wearing a nice suit, smoking a cigar. "I look like Groucho Marx," he chuckles. (Comments like these, referring to Groucho Marx, show that the current personality is tracking everything that's going on in session. It's as if a client runs a dual consciousness during the session.) He's in the castle at Dubrovnik. Even though it's cold with its marble floors and he'd rather live in the village, as governor he must live here.

I suggest he jump forward to about age thirty. He is still in power and feels he's done a good job as governor. Everyone is content, but you can still see the effects of the war on the outskirts of town. "It's a constant reminder of what we don't want. I leave it this way to remind us of the lessons of history," he explains. Otherwise things appear to be peaceful.

"I still talk to Dad in my mind," he continues. "He's like an adviser to me, but even more so now than when he was alive. We're so close, yet not together."

I instruct the governor to jump ahead to age forty. He sees a picture of himself hanging on the wall in a warm room with tapestries. He has put on weight and sports a handlebar mustache that curls up at the ends. But it's just his portrait. "I'm not there—I'm not alive anymore!" he realizes. Understanding this, I move him back to his last day in that life.

"They kill me—the nationalists kill me!" He is surprised. Although most people are happy with his rule, it turns out that a man who served as his trusted assistant for many years unexpectedly assassinates him. "I'm sitting in my power chair, and he takes a sword and runs it through the back of the chair, all the way through my back," he says. It is only a few years later; he's thirty-two years old at the time of his death. He identifies his trusted assistant turned assassin as a man who has been a business associate in Richard's current life.

At his death, our governor floats up on a cloud, describing it like an out-of-body experience. Dad is waiting for him: "Where've you been?" he jokes.

The most salient lesson Richard draws from this lifetime actually focuses on the need to slow down, relax, and cherish the good times. In fact, his need to rest includes finding a place where he can get out of cell phone range! After that, being strong and working hard to right a wrong, rather than giving in, is another important lesson. When consulting his higher guidance, Richard is told that it is important to trust his own wisdom and intuition, especially when others are pressuring him; he can move away from their chatter and negativity to find his own truth. He also receives confirmation that the birthmark on his chest was indeed carried over from the sword that was run through his body in that prior life.

Richard asks his guidance where Dad is now. "Stick a fork in me—

I'm done," his father says on showing up, using one of his typical, corny responses. Dad indicates he is ready to take a break from the human plane and also has rest on his agenda, just as Richard should.

———

I found Richard's story very touching. There was such harmony and closeness in the relationship between these two fighting men that they decided to return as father and son in another life. Yet they have continued to be plagued with physical separation all too soon in their lives together. It would be interesting to investigate their relationship further and see what originally set up this "close but not together" dynamic. I have no doubt that the two of them will be finding each other again in another life.

This regression is also a wonderful example of how a client can have a significant regression experience even when he has no prior exposure to past life work and doesn't really know what to expect, other than having a wife tell him, "You should do this too!" It was a true pleasure to work with Richard and help him to connect in an even more meaningful way with his father.

The laughter continued into our wrap-up. When Natalie arrived at my office to pick up Richard, she blurted out excitedly, "Did you find out about the birthmark?" Richard and I looked at each other and broke out laughing. I figured the somewhat long answer would make a great story for him to tell her on their way home.

ESSENTIAL TRUTHS UNCOVERED

* Remembering the mistakes of our history so we don't repeat them.
* Slowing down to cherish the good times.
* Calling upon strength and courage to correct wrongs.
* Trusting your own intuition and wisdom.
* Enjoying life through laughter.

EXPANDING YOUR PERSPECTIVE

Since Richard had traveled to Croatia, a skeptic could say that he made this story up from his imagination because he was familiar with the area and fond of the country. On the other hand, perhaps he was drawn to Croatia in his current life because he was already familiar with it and had worked so hard to improve the lives of the Croatian people in a past life.

Paying attention to the areas of the world that hold a fascination for you, or those areas that you have no interest in ever seeing, may provide you with clues to your own prior lifetimes. (Those places in which we are strongly disinterested might actually indicate that we had a life experience there that was very unpleasant.) Where have you already traveled, and what's still on your bucket list as a must-see?

Your journal would be a good place to list all the areas of the world that you have traveled to and what your reaction was to each area. Is there somewhere you felt instantly at home? Were there places that you couldn't get away from soon enough? Did you have any experiences of déjà vu in any of these locations? Allow yourself to daydream about the possibilities in each location.

On your travels in the future, decide now to open your awareness and invite images and memories to come forward. You just might get some glimpses or inclinations of past times spent there.

CHAPTER 13

Our Relationships Transcend Time

IT'S QUITE COMMON that the first thing that piques people's interest in investigating past lives is a question about a current relationship. Relationship dynamics can be so challenging, and despite whatever we try, we often can't seem to get past a repeating pattern. Where did that pattern come from? How do we break its hold on us? Or we meet someone with whom we feel an instant connection, causing us to wonder when and in what circumstances we have known that individual in the past. Often the question comes from a need to reconnect with someone we have lost, either through death or separation. We want to be reassured that we have been with that loved one before and, therefore, we can rest in the knowledge that we will be with him/her again in the future.

From everything I have learned as a past life therapist, we tend to travel in groups. Most people in the field refer to a "soul group," a group of souls with whom we have a strong connection and with whom we choose to reincarnate into a similar time and place so we can be together on the human plane. Usually this is because of a strong love connection. At times we may find that these are the individuals who also challenge us the most; most likely we have agreed on a soul level to come together to work out negative dynamics or to help each other with important areas of personal growth. Beyond our core soul group, however, we will also reencounter many of the lesser players in our personal dramas across the ages. It's fairly unusual to find someone who plays a truly significant role in your life, be it positive or negative, whom you have not encountered sometime before.

It's intriguing to see how the relationships change. In one lifetime we might be husband and wife, in another master and slave, in another business rivals, and in another parent and child. We swap genders. We swap family positions. We swap power and influence with each other. But we often see a similar dynamic arising no matter what the official profile of the relationship. Often we are working on a destructive pattern or issue until we can get it right, do it differently. And sometimes we are souls who have such a strong love connection that we just want to be together again in happiness and harmony.

This brings up the question of soul mates. This term is used quite often by clients and in the general population to mean the one unique individual who you are meant to be with, often across multiple lifetimes. Is there really such a thing as a unique soul mate, an eternal one? I believe the term "soul mate," as it is conventionally used, is a bit misinterpreted. It is actually possible for most of us to renew deep, abiding love relationships with many different partners from our past lives. If encountered at the right time and in the right place, it's quite possible that we have more than one soul mate in this lifetime. (Thank goodness, because—given the billions of people on the planet—finding that one unique individual could be a very daunting task!) No matter what our initial plan upon entering this lifetime, human choice may change the course of our lives. This can bring us down different paths and expose us to a variety of people, with the opportunity to renew deep connections from the past that may have been only an outside possibility otherwise.

Even so, it does seem that at times some people do come in with the specific intent of renewing a romantic love relationship from the past. This is most often seen when the dynamic was unable to complete itself fully in the prior lifetime. So in that sense we might consider an individual to truly be our intended soul mate, and when we have fulfilled that relationship, or when we want a different experience or type of learning, we will probably choose another partner.

Although we do tend to travel with members of our soul group, there can be gaps of time between the lifetimes we share. Especially if we subscribe to the concept that eternal time is not linear, it does not matter that a couple of centuries on the physical plane may elapse before we are together again. We are all weaving multiple threads in the tapestries of our earth journeys, and we may work on one for a while, then set that down and focus on another—possibly multiple others—before returning to the first thread. And at times we also complete a thread relating to a specific other soul. Our work with each other is done, our business is finished, and particularly if it has been a negative or destructive dynamic, we don't have to do that anymore!

Here is a sampling of relationship issues that clients have brought in over the years. Not surprisingly, it is predominantly women who come in with this focus. The men who have consulted me on relationship-specific questions have equally interesting stories; however, this just doesn't come up as often with men.

Father of Her Child

A young woman had a son by a jazz musician who lived across the country. She still hoped they might have a future together and wanted to know about the history between the two of them. She went to a lifetime of wealth and luxury where they both survived the sinking of the *Titanic* and eventually had a long and happy married life together. She felt reassured that there might be a possibility of a happy ending in this life too.

Destructive Dynamics

A woman wanted to look at prior life connections with her mother, whom she described as being emotionally abusive. She went to a lifetime as a young woman in the early 1800s in Romania. At age fifteen she was given in an arranged marriage to an older man for whom she was expected to keep house and to serve sexually. This husband (her mother in the current life) would drink and become physically abusive to her. After dying a bitter, childless old woman, she came to see in the afterlife that her husband had never been loved or cared for; no one had taught him how to love. She came to a level of forgiveness toward her mother's prior and present personality.

Treated Like a Slave

A woman described her family dynamics as follows: "I feel like a slave in my own family; I do everything for everyone else." She experienced her life as nonstop work, and even now, when she was in her thirties, her father would regularly borrow money from her. She wanted to understand the source of this dynamic.

She went to a lifetime in the 1870s in a Mediterranean country where, as an illegitimate child, she was taken in by relatives. Her role was to care for everyone else's needs. "There is no happiness for me," she said. "I owe them." Some of the adoptive family members were now members of her current family. In processing the lifetime, she was told that it was time to challenge family tradition and transform her current situation.

Together Again

A young woman wanted to learn more about the depth of love and connection she felt with her boyfriend. In one lifetime in early Greece, as a member of the royal family, she fell in love with a soldier (whom we identified as her current boyfriend). The family had him killed and she herself committed suicide as a result. In another lifetime in India they were a happily married couple. He died while still young, promising her that they would be together again.

Releasing Old Ties

A male client wanted to look at any unfinished karmic business he might have with his former girlfriend to help him fully let go of the relationship. In the life we visited, he was a miner obsessed with finding the mother lode. He died in a mining accident due to his own carelessness. As a result, he left his wife (former girlfriend in his current life) and two small children without resources. The key message he uncovered was the importance of being there for family and dropping his obsession with money and success.

Fear of Relationship

More than one client has wanted to look at a generalized fear of a committed relationship. Not surprisingly, this typically springs from heartrending losses in the past. One woman went to a lifetime as a blacksmith in Bosnia about the year 1820. Soldiers arrived, and the blacksmith hesitated to stop their aggressive behavior. The situation turned ugly, and the soldiers ended up raping and killing his wife and daughter. When he finally tried to act, it was too late. He eventually drank himself to death out of guilt and remorse.

Another client visited a Native American lifetime in which she lost her husband, two sons, and eventually her own life to white men. She was told by her higher guidance that she and her husband would eventually reconnect in this lifetime. Her daughter and her ex-husband in this life were also family members from the Native American lifetime.

My Husband's Friend

A young woman was torn by her sense of connection with a friend of her husband who lived in another country. She wanted to understand the strength of these feelings. She visited a lifetime as a farmwife in Pennsylvania in the 1930s. Her husband then, the same person as her husband now, was singularly uncommunicative and distant—just as he was now. His friend showed up as her son, with whom she had a very close and loving relationship. She was told by her higher guidance that they had shared many lifetimes together, but in this life their paths were meant to diverge.

A Ten-Year Affair

After an affair with a married man had lasted ten years, this client struggled with trying to break it off. She wanted to look at any prior lifetimes together in the hopes of breaking the dynamic. She visited an Irish lifetime in the 1700s where, as a healer, she was accused of witchcraft. There was a military man (the current lover) who fancied her, but he didn't step forward to defend her until it was too late. She was burned alive.

In another life, she was a female ruler in ancient Egypt, and he was her consort. Although she actually loved him, she treated him heartlessly because she believed, as a ruler, to show love would be to show weakness. This is a good example of a destructive pattern being traded back and forth between two parties. The client was given the guidance that her lesson for this life was to learn to express love and then to let go and move on.

Shall I Leave Him?

A woman came in looking for clarity in deciding whether to leave her husband. She described him as disconnected from the family, critical, and abusive with his language. She uncovered a Native American lifetime in which her spouse died at a young age, although it was not the same individual as her current husband. However, in this case, she found a fulfilling life on her own and adopted orphaned children. Her guidance told her that her focus in this lifetime was meant to be her son. She was also told that she needed to be brutally honest with her husband regarding what he needed to change in order for her to stay in the marriage.

At Arm's Length

A man who had been recently divorced consulted me about a new relationship he had formed over the Internet. Despite a number of plans to meet in person, he kept finding ways to avoid it, although he also felt unwilling to break off the relationship. He wanted to address his tendency to keep this new love interest at arm's length. He went to a life in England in the 1600s in which his wife died quite young and left him with a young daughter. He was so grief stricken that he kept his daughter (his recently divorced wife) at considerable emotional distance thereafter. Spiritual guidance counseled him to focus on the hurt that was never healed. Doing so would address his distancing problem.

Torn Between Two Men

A woman consulted me about her inability to choose between her former boyfriend and the new man in her life. She felt quite a bit of guilt about leaving her ex. She visited a lifetime as a frontiersman in the American West who died fighting in the Indian Wars in Montana. At the time of his death, he was sorry for abandoning his wife (identified as the new man now), but he especially felt tremendous guilt about leaving his son fatherless. This son was identified as the ex-boyfriend now. We also found her together with the ex-boyfriend in a Roman lifetime in which the client refused his marriage proposal and ended up feeling guilty and responsible for the man's deep unhappiness. Spiritual guidance centered on releasing the guilt toward the ex-boyfriend from the prior lives and eliminating that from the client's current problem of deciding between the two men.

Understanding My Husband

A woman who had been married for thirty-five years to the same man still struggled with aspects of his personality. She wanted to see a prior lifetime together that was happy and fulfilled, to help inspire her about their connection. She went to a lifetime before recorded history in southeastern Eurasia where widespread travel and trading were just developing. As a fabric maker, she was enthralled with the stories of other places, other peoples and customs, other languages. Her key entry to these new aspects of the world was her husband's twin brother (her current husband), who had traveled widely and was known as a wise man. She spent hours talking with him, and they had a special closeness that she treasured. After the session, the client felt a new sense of her husband's value in her life.

————

With my training in marriage and family therapy, I was taught to focus on the interactions between people, how our internal dynamics impact our interpersonal relationships. Of course, it's vital to pay close attention to this aspect of our lives. Our relationships can bring the most profound rewards and sometimes the most heartbreaking difficulties. It has been very rewarding for me to be able to help past life clients release relationship challenges more quickly than I saw with conventional therapeutic approaches. The following three chapters are detailed examples of how dynamics set up in prior lifetimes can influence a client's current life and relationships.

EXPANDING YOUR PERSPECTIVE

Look at the key relationships in your life. If you had to guess, who do you think is a member of your core soul group? Generally, members of our soul groups are the people we feel the most warmth and connection with, the people we feel naturally at home with. But sometimes certain members of our core soul groups can also be the people who give us the most trouble because they are helping us to grow emotionally or spiritually or to overcome an old pattern. Soul group members can show up as our spouses, parents, children, grandchildren, siblings, teachers, friends, or coworkers. Broaden your vision of the people in your life by imagining how you may have been together before. What might be the reason you are in each other's lives again? What potentials for personal growth lie within your relationships?

CHAPTER 14

Hanging on to a Happy Past

VIVIAN WASN'T particularly happy with her profession. She felt unacknowledged at work, but although she was angry about this, she felt that it was really no different from the treatment that her coworkers received. She had been divorced seventeen years earlier and had two adult daughters, who were quite independent. Vivian asserted that she actively reinforced their independence from her. In fact, she seemed determined to keep her connections limited, describing herself as having few friends.

About fifteen months earlier, Vivian felt that she had undergone a bit of a personality change, growing more cynical and even less friendly with others. She attributed this to the deaths of four people who had been very important to her: her best friend, two aunts with whom she had been quite close, and a woman she had always considered her "second mom." This was quite a list of recent losses.

Vivian described her experience of life as "living *Groundhog Day* every day," with a feeling of being held back somehow from engaging in life. "My dad always said I was born in the wrong time," she shared. "And I was too bright for a female." She seemed to have some minor psychic abilities: as an adolescent she had seen ghost-like images of people she felt she knew. She also described a prophetic sense about her father's death. She had done some earlier work in hypnosis in which she experienced visions of scenes in China, with which she had felt a strong connection. Additionally, she had been very frightened by some images of the Old West, which she described as scenes of "cowboys and Indians." Vivian believed that she had been "horribly wounded sometime in a past life" and that this was holding her back from enjoying her current life. I decided to use the phrase "whatever is holding you back from enjoying and fully participating in this life" as our entry point into past life work.

———

It takes a little while for Vivian to ease into the session. This is not surprising, given her expectation that she is going to see a lifetime in which she was horribly wounded. Rather than entering a scene from a prior life, she initially sees circles of blue light out of which emerges the figure of a man. He is old, with no hair, and Vivian recognizes him. "He comes to me at times," she says. When I ask what his purpose is, she replies: "To protect me." This is very helpful, and I suggest to Vivian that she bring him along for protection during the session.

Vivian is now able to enter a lifetime. Her first impression is of pretty gold slippers, soft and comfortable. She is dressed in beautiful clothes: a creamy-white, flowing silk dress with long sleeves. Her dark hair is done up in a fancy coiffure. She feels carefree, with no problems. She guesses that she must be wealthy and cared for, and realizes that she is still quite young, about twelve.

I move our attention to her surroundings. The girl is in a bright room with windows. "It's my parlor," she says. She is sitting alone in a chair by the windows, with a cat on her lap. "It feels good here," she remarks happily. After some questioning, she identifies the year to be 1791 and the country to be Belgium. The name she goes by is Clarissa.

I direct Clarissa to the last meal that she had. It's breakfast that morning, being taken in a formal dining room. There is a woman at the head of the table, her grandmother. "She's very strong and a little scary," the girl says, but there is a strong sense of connection. We are able to identify this woman as one of the beloved aunts who died recently in Vivian's lifetime.

"I love it here. I don't want to go!" Clarissa exclaims. "I love the clothes and the things she's given me. But I have to go away."

There are others in the room as well. She sees an older brother. She says that their relationship isn't the greatest and he's glad she's going away. But she loves him nonetheless, and we are able to identify him as Vivian's brother in her current life.

Standing by a chair in the dining room is a man she knows is her uncle. Again the relationship is not stellar: "We think differently," Clarissa explains. "I'm eclectic in my thinking; he's strict and close-minded. We butt heads." We are able to identify this man as the same soul as an uncle in Vivian's current life.

I probe into why Clarissa is living here, with these relatives. She explains that her parents died when she was about two years old, and she and her brother came to live with her grandmother and her uncle. Now she is being sent away to school "to learn to be a lady. But I'm scared," she says. "I like to run and play and I will miss my cat!" Being strong-willed like her grandmother and uncle, she argues her case but is unable to change their minds.

I have Clarissa move forward to the next significant event in her life, expecting we may see some scenes at school. Instead we move on to her marriage. She's about twenty years old now, finished with formal education. "I changed a lot," she observes, "reined in my spirit. I made some friends and minded the teachers."

This is an arranged marriage. Clarissa doesn't know him well "but he seems nice," she allows. Her grandmother selected her husband-to-be, saying, "Trust me. He will be good to you." Clarissa acquiesces to the marriage, accepting her grandmother's choice for her. Her new husband is a little older than she is, not extremely wealthy but quite comfortable financially, and he will be able to give her the easy life to which she is accustomed. However, over time, she becomes disenchanted with him. "He's cold," she says. "I can't see his soul. I'm just an ornament for his image."

We move forward to the next significant event. She now has a daughter. "She's my friend," Clarissa states. "We go shopping together; it's lovely and we're happy." Her husband is not in the picture emotionally, but it no longer seems to bother her. We are able to identify her daughter as an old high school friend in Vivian's current life. We move forward to the time when Clarissa's daughter is getting married. She is permitted to choose her own husband. Clarissa likes him, and she is happy that the new couple will be living nearby.

The next major event involves much turmoil and stress. "I'm strong, standing before the townsfolk," she realizes. "They need me. There's been a fire, and they've lost their homes. They need help." Clarissa is obviously very distressed by the plight of the people of the town: "There are so many of them; it is so sad. I've done charity work, but this is overwhelming. It bothers me so much that I get sick. I don't have enough to help them all, and the sadness is pulling me down." She realizes that she is actually dying.

We go to her death scene. She is in bed at home. Her daughter is there, as is her son-in-law and her older brother. Her relationship with her brother continued to be challenging at times, but she now understands him as always just needing to go his own way. "I'm going to miss them all so much. I love them so much. I don't want to go!" she cries. Clarissa recognizes that she's dying from a heart condition. Her chest feels heavy and she can't breathe well. "I had a good life," she observes. "I've been very kind, very loving." Yet she's afraid of dying, fearing there will be nothing afterwards. At the time of death, she experiences a bright, intense white light that she floats into. She describes the feeling as if she's being pulled into a soft, velvety bubble.

As we process the lifetime after the death, Vivian identifies some important lessons. Learning to compromise is the first to come forth: "I didn't get to do what I really wanted—travel and see the world—

but I had a fulfilling life even though it was a compromise." The importance of helping others was also key: "I was in a position to help others. It's not about the dictates of your religion; it's about what's in your heart."

Vivian relates themes from Clarissa's life to her current life. She notes how, as in the past, she relates better to women than to men, and feels she still fights the tendency of men to want to dominate. She battles with the feeling that she is not seen as a real person, just "a thing," as Clarissa experienced with her husband. Vivian is surprised by the number of people from that lifetime who have played important roles again in her current life. Clearly she did not want to lose them, even if the relationships were sometimes less than ideal. The spirit of the older man, her protector, moves in with healing energy, and a deep sense of peacefulness descends on Vivian as she releases that lifetime.

I continued to see Vivian for a few months for follow-up work and more conventional counseling to help integrate her past life experiences more fully. We explored her family-of-origin dynamics in her current life, the painful losses of loved ones, and the patterns she saw that were reflected in her regression. She felt more empowered after the regression and began to engage more with her life. She made some important decisions for herself, including selecting a location out of state where she wanted to retire in a few years and actually purchasing a house there. She found herself dealing calmly and assertively with a man at work whom she had always found very imposing. And by the end of the few months we spent in counseling, she had quit her job and was feeling great about it. She no longer felt stuck in *Groundhog Day*; that was evident!

I wanted to share this regression story because it demonstrates a couple of key factors. One is that not all past life regression experiences are filled with huge trauma. Overall, Clarissa had a happy, comfortable, and fulfilled life. Sure, there were some of the normal challenges with human relationships, but she loved the people in her life and her biggest challenge was leaving them at her death. In fact, that appeared to be an important factor that was impacting Vivian's life. She was stuck when she came to see me, not able to move forward. In a sense, her not moving forward was Vivian's protest and the expression of her desire to stay in the happy past with the people she loved. I believe this issue was particularly reactivated when she experienced the separation from loved ones in her current life with the close deaths of four important people.

When we have lost a loved one, it can be wonderfully healing to find them in prior lifetimes. It assures us that we have been together before, we will be together again, and the bonds of love are not lost. Clearly the many figures in Clarissa's life in Belgium were here again in Vivian's life to help put to rest the feelings of loss and the unwillingness to move on.

It seems some of the conditioning from Belgium in the late 1700s was still at work for Vivian: making compromises to have a comfortable life, following the status quo, turning over the direction of her life to other authority figures, be it a grandmother or a male figure. It was wonderfully rewarding to see how quickly Vivian began to move forward again and to start making empowering choices for herself. She even described her self-care as now "giving myself exactly what I want; the key is to be myself!" Enough compromise, perhaps, and time to live the life she wanted for herself. After all, she was an independent woman in the twenty-first century and no longer had to acquiesce to another's dictates for her life. She did a wonderful job of taking charge of her own destiny.

ESSENTIAL TRUTHS UNCOVERED

* Valuing compromise when necessary.
* Helping others when you are in a position to do so.

∗ Making sacrifices from a heart-centered place, not from obligation or social expectations.

∗ Taking responsibility for your own life. Don't abdicate control to authority figures.

EXPANDING YOUR PERSPECTIVE

When we feel like something is holding us back from engaging fully in our current lives, it's interesting to ponder whether it's because we don't want to let go of something particularly wonderful that we've experienced in the past. One thing we can count on in life is that things change, yet the human condition is such that we tend to resist and sometimes fight the changes. This can prevent new, exciting things from developing.

Are there any areas in your life where you've been resisting change? Can you turn that resistance into gratitude for what you've had in the past, and open yourself up to new surprises that might be in store for the future? What would it take for you to decide to trust your higher consciousness, or the universe to guide you and provide what you need for your next steps in life? Are you blocking new directions in your life by refusing to let go and flow with the natural order of change?

CHAPTER 15

Fighting for My Life

DR. BRIAN WEISS referred Tamara to me, back in the day when he maintained an active referral list of past life therapists who had trained with him. In her mid-thirties, Tamara worked in the high-tech industry and described herself as a very results-oriented person. Tamara was quite intrigued when she read two of Dr. Weiss's books while vacationing. Upon returning home, she decided to pursue a regression session for herself.

Tamara wanted to look at the dynamics with her husband, Brad, whom she had known for only about four years. She felt that the two of them were continually engaged in a power struggle and that she needed to defend herself from being overpowered by him. Her phrase that best described her experience was "like fighting for my life." When a client comes up with a rich, dramatic simile like this, I have found that it very often indicates a strong dynamic at play from a prior lifetime. Tamara had meditated fairly regularly in the past and had done other work in hypnosis about a year earlier. I anticipated that she would be a fairly easy subject to work with. We entered the regression looking for the lifetime she had shared with Brad that underlay their power struggle and that "fighting for my life" feeling.

The first impression Tamara receives is of wearing sandals with metal armor on the fronts of the shins, stopping just below the knee. She is in a male body. He is wearing a long shirt made of a rough material with metal armor over it. On his head is a metal helmet that comes to a small point at the top, but it is open at the face. He has wavy dark brown hair that is about shoulder length, and he sports a beard and mustache. He describes himself as Roman, a career soldier in his early forties, and says he goes by a name that sounds something like "Thor."

We turn our attention to Thor's surroundings. He is in a desert-like area with dry, cracked ground. It's mostly flat but with some hills and feels like foreign territory to him. Eventually he is able to identify the area as Egypt, and he's part of an expedition on a fact-finding mission. At present, though, he is alone. "I'm feeling anxious, like I'm not supposed to be here," he comments. "I'm trying to leave, get away. I saw an event—I wasn't a part of it— and I feel in danger."

I ask Thor to go to the event itself to see what happened. It's an argument between two fellow soldiers that turns violent. He doesn't feel he knows either combatant well. One soldier kills the other, but Thor is not able to get a clear picture of either man's face at this point.

Suddenly he has the sensation of a heavy weight on his head and chest. He feels paralyzed; he can't move. "Something fell on me. I'm pinned down," he realizes. "Stones—a part of a building? I'm alone; I don't know where I am."

It's not clear to me whether we have jumped to the end of Thor's lifetime or if the client has switched to another lifetime, as sometimes happens. I redirect our focus back to the Roman life in case we have switched. "What is important for us to see about Thor's life?" I ask.

More details of the story begin to unfold. "The murderer—he was highly ranked. He knew I had seen what happened. He accused me of having committed the murder instead. I'm taken to trial in Rome on this trumped-up charge!"

Tamara's husband Brad's former identity suddenly appears. "He's the judge—the ultimate decision maker!" Thor exclaims. "I feel like he's biased against me for some reason; it's not bribery but just personal distaste." The judge finds him guilty and sentences him to death by beheading.

As I continue to probe, more information about the dynamic between Thor and the judge opens up. They knew each other in childhood. "I was a bully," Thor admits. "He caught the brunt of it. We were never friends. From my perspective it was just fun to bully him."

After sentencing, Thor is imprisoned before his execution. He requests to talk to the judge again. "I try to plead my case one more time. He's callous, cold. I only have a few days left," Thor laments. At the moment of execution, Thor is trembling with anxiety, fear, and sorrow. He observes how he created this situation so long ago, unaware, as a callous youth himself. "I should keep my head down, keep my mouth shut, mind my own business," he concludes. He struggles until he's been positioned with his hands and head locked down, screaming his innocence of the murder of which he's been accused, up to the very end. The executioner's blade swings down. His spirit goes rapidly to a peaceful place.

As we look at the lessons from Thor's lifetime, having humility and feeling respect for other people come up as key issues. "These were missing from that personality," Tamara notices. Another lesson is about honesty: "Honesty may not always be believed and may not keep you out of trouble. It may not always be the best policy!"

We look at how she was literally fighting for her life with Brad in their Roman personalities. Although Brad was the judge who condemned her, she had set it up by bullying him in their youth. Tamara notes that, in her current life, as a child she was hypersensitive to bullying. She also reflects on the issue of honesty and how she has had to struggle with that within herself in this lifetime.

Tamara's higher guidance indicates to her that there is more work to be done in regard to cleaning up past life dynamics with Brad. She is told that there has been a chain of wrongdoings against each other over multiple lifetimes. In particular, a Middle Eastern lifetime is described in which a romantic betrayal is involved. As we wind up the session, Tamara and I talk about the need to keep her arguments with Brad in the present time, to learn to talk herself down from being highly activated as if she were again in a life-threatening situation with him, rather than merely having a disagreement with a spouse.

———

About a month later I received an e-mail from Tamara. "I'm not sure exactly how to explain what I've noticed," she wrote, "but I feel things have shifted a bit for me. It seems like there is less of a need to be confrontational with Brad. I don't always need to argue every single point like I used to. I seem to be able to reflect on certain situations first before reacting emotionally like before."

Feeling that she wanted to do more work, she requested another session. When we met again, Tamara reiterated that she felt she had made progress in choosing her battles and was more aware before she reacted. However, she observed that she distrusted Brad's judgment in regard to her own physical safety. She particularly noticed this when engaged in athletic activities together. Brad was quite a risk taker, and would push her to go beyond the limits of what she considered to be safe. We did agree, however, to focus on the Middle Eastern lifetime that had come up at the end of her last session. Perhaps it would also address Tamara's sense that Brad did not give enough thought to her physical safety.

———

Once again, Tamara finds herself wearing sandals. They are dusty, made of brown leather, and strapped up to the ankles. And once again she is in a male body. His legs are bare, and he is wearing a long robe of a thick, woven material that is itchy to the skin. Its design is simple: it hangs free, with sleeves to the elbow. He has a rust-colored turban on his head. He is about forty-five years old, has very dark brown weathered skin, dark brown eyes, and a close-cropped black beard.

He is standing in his village. There are simple huts made of mud, with straw roofs. It is windy and dusty. He is outside his house, holding a walking stick and gazing toward the edge of the valley, toward the mountains. "I'm looking for something," he remarks. His family is inside the hut: two young boys, ages four and two. "I care very much for them," he says sadly. "I'm concerned for the future. I'm sad for my family and me. Their mother is gone!"

We bring his wife into focus. "She was very unhappy with me and our life. I was aware of it, but I didn't think she'd leave," he reflects. "I made her unhappy with the other women I spent time with. I was unfaithful to her. But it's very common," he justifies. They argued about the other women, but he claims he didn't realize she saw it differently from the way most other wives in the community did. Apparently it was seen as normal and expected that most husbands had their dalliances with other women.

As we look at his wife more closely, he describes her as having very dark brown hair and green eyes and as being quite a bit younger than he is. She's pretty and in her early twenties. (We check, but she doesn't seem to be someone from Tamara's current lifetime.) Their marriage was arranged. The families knew each other, and her father was adamant that the two of them marry. Our reluctant bridegroom describes feeling that he had no real choice; there was so much pressure from the girl's father.

"I cared for her but didn't love her," he says. "She's pretty but not my choice." There is actually a slightly older sister that he had his heart set upon. "She has similar feelings toward me, but their father is a very powerful force, and he insists on the younger sister. I sever my relationship with the older sister when I get married," he says sadly. (We take a moment to see if this older sister is someone Tamara recognizes, and she says the energy is similar to a fellow she dated some years ago.)

His father-in-law is playing such a prominent role that I decide we need to learn a little more about him. He's in his late sixties, wealthy, and respected in the community. "My father was not alive at the time," our bridegroom observes, "so what he [the father-in-law] says goes." I ask if he is familiar, and a little surprisingly he is identified as Brad. The two men have a strained relationship. "I asked for the older daughter in marriage," he recalls, "but he is not open to our love. He makes it clear he's in control." The younger man is angry and rebels against this powerless position he feels he's been thrown into. This is what drives his philandering. He doesn't fathom until his wife actually leaves him that his infidelity might lead to some serious ramifications.

"The word's out! I know her father is coming after me. I'm afraid I'll be killed by him," he says anxiously. Once again he expresses fear about his children's welfare. He's sad and angry but feels he was robbed of having a choice. "I can get out of my life finally," he says resentfully.

We move to the conclusion of this situation. The father-in-law rides up with four or five men. By this point our philandering husband is no longer fearful; he's just angry. At the same time he feels resigned to his fate. The men tie his arms and legs, throw him over the back of a horse, and take him to the center of the village, where he is hanged.

"This is very inconsistent with the usual attitudes toward extramarital affairs," our victim insists to the end, "but he [the father-in-law] rules, so no one questions it. Early on, I decided I would never let him control me on the inside, despite appearances. I don't kick or scream; I just go with it. I don't care." With death the personality realizes a freedom and awareness that he did not recognize while alive. "I succumbed to someone I didn't have to," he observes. "I took the path of least resistance."

We move forward to process this lifetime further. "Honor yourself and your own heart instead of another's forceful nature. Make life decisions for yourself" is an important lesson that first emerges. "The minute you stop listening to yourself, you stop living your life."

Tamara continues with other observations: "Don't compromise what you really want, or you'll end up really unhappy. People are looking out for their own best interests, not particularly trying to hurt yours, but be aware that their and your interests are not always compatible." Some tough but very practical advice on life and looking out for yourself.

When I probe into how the dynamics of that Middle Eastern life relate to her current life, Tamara believes that all the lessons directly correlate with the here and now. She describes feeling inferior, not able to make good decisions, as if others know more. This self-doubt in the face of a strong other, as in the lifetime just visited, resonates strongly for her. "Brad's emotional power over me from the past needs to be severed," she concludes.

When we pull in higher guidance, this theme continues. "Start to listen to your intuition: Stay open to your feelings; stay connected to them," she is told. "It will tell you if you are on track if you listen and feel. This applies to every aspect of your life, including your work and your purpose. If you connect to your heart and feeling, your purpose will be apparent and will unfold. If you stay in your head, it will elude you."

I work with Tamara on that energetic connection between Brad and herself. She sees it in her mind's eye as a slimy, murky green cord that connects to her stomach just below the belly button—the second chakra level, which has to do with personal power, sex, money, relationships, and defining boundaries. She feels the connection is fear based now, but there would be no power to it if either of them could transcend the fear. We use the image of a very bright white laser light to sever the fear connection, cutting the cord and sealing both ends. The cord ends burn into particles and dissipate. In the cord's stead, I have Tamara imagine a new connection, reaching from heart to heart, that is based on love, mutual respect, and trust. She sees it as a pulsating beam of light, iridescent opal in color. I suggest that she continue to use this imagery on her own in the following days and weeks, focusing in her meditation time on the laser eliminating the fear connection and on the iridescent heart beam that forges a new, healthier, and happier connection between her and Brad.

———

I think it would be safe to conclude that Tamara's feeling that Brad did not have enough concern about her physical safety was related to losing her life at his hands in these prior lifetimes. Although his approach to sports activities may have been more daring than hers, she was undoubtedly overreacting, thanks to the filter of these past life experiences. During the sessions, Tamara saw glimpses of other lifetimes between herself and her husband: a lifetime in Scotland or England, where they were a couple, and a lifetime in Egypt, where there was a master-slave relationship with—guess what?—more power issues. When we see repeating dynamics such as this, in which there is continued conflict and injury between parties, it typically can be traced back in a series of many lifetimes. However, it's usually not necessary to track down every instance, every lifetime, in which the dynamics were played out.

With these two regressions, the nature of the problem that was impacting Tamara's marriage today was well exhibited. Specific work was done to clear that out and begin to forge a new basis for their interactions. Obviously there was a strong connection between the two of them, and they continued to come together to learn how to work with each other in love and cooperation rather than in conflict and constant power struggles. This is a good example of souls agreeing to work on a particular issue together across lifetimes—even when it may mean a lot of trouble on the physical plane—for the growth of each party involved.

I think Tamara's story is a good demonstration of the way in which we change places with other members of our soul group—those individuals with whom we have strong connections and with whom we reincarnate over and over. Spouses in this lifetime, Tamara and her husband were childhood bully and victim and then prisoner and condemning judge in Rome; philandering husband and controlling father-in-law in the Middle East; spouses in Scotland; and master and slave in Egypt—and they probably shared other relationship dynamics across the ages. I believe this also may show why most of us come into this life with the veil drawn across our knowledge of what has happened in the past. If these dynamics from prior lifetimes had been known in advance, Tamara may very likely have avoided getting into a relationship with Brad altogether, thus cheating the couple of the opportunity to work through and heal the unhealthy aspects of their relationship.

A quick note about Tamara's guidance on work and life purpose: this was not something she brought up with me when discussing her intention to do past life work. However, it is often the case that clients have other agendas and questions that they don't necessarily share with me initially. Part of this is because I encourage them to try to focus on one issue so we can be effective in our work together. I also know that if something is important for clients to see or be told, it will get through to them. And this often comes during that time when we are consulting their higher guidance toward the end of the regression. I take a very expansive approach to this part of our work, asking what the clients' guidance wants them to know, and suggesting that they pose any question at all that they might have. This is often when tidbits—like Tamara's advice on allowing her purpose to unfold by tuning in to her intuition and feelings—can come forth.

ESSENTIAL TRUTHS UNCOVERED

* Having humility yourself, and respect for others.
* Making decisions for yourself rather than taking the path of least resistance.
* Listening to your heart and feelings to guide your life path.

EXPANDING YOUR PERSPECTIVE

We've all had difficult relationships; it seems like that's part and par-cel of being human. I invite you to take a closer look at a relationship that you see as problematic. What is this relationship challenging you to learn? Is it blocking your growth, or is it causing you to stretch your limits, your image of yourself, or your idea of the ways things or people should be? Could part of the difficulty be in the way you have reacted to the situation? If you changed your reaction, do you think the dynamic would change? Would you benefit more from walking away from the situation or from mastering it? There is an appropriate time for each. How would your life be different without this person in your life?

CHAPTER 16

Accepting Life and Death

ONE OF THE MOST heartrending experiences for me as a therapist is when a parent comes in seeking connection with a child he/she has lost to death. Ruth's experience was one that still brings tears to my eyes. Her beloved daughter, Susie, had died a year earlier as a result of medical treatment gone wrong. Ruth was still deeply grieving this loss and felt that she was no longer engaging well with the rest of her family. She was searching for some relief from her grief and greater understanding of why this had happened. Rather than spend a lot of time gathering further information on Ruth's current life, we moved pretty quickly into the regression work.

Ruth's first impression is of bare feet on soft, sandy soil, and bare legs. She is in a female body and is wrapped in a yellow-colored, very soft and light fabric that leaves one shoulder bare and is tied around the waist. She describes herself as having "dark skin, a flat nose, slanted eyes, dark long hair," which is loosely tied back with what she thinks is grass. She is about twenty years old and feels strong and healthy.

I direct her to focus on her surroundings. The young woman is working on the beach. She senses greenery behind her, and white sand. "Well, I'm supposed to be working," she admits, "but I'm not really, more goofing around." Along with two of her brothers, she is gathering vegetation that has been drying under the trees at the edge of the beach. One brother is about fifteen or sixteen years old and tall. They are teasing each other a lot. The other brother is a couple years younger, rounder, not as tall. She says that she is not as close with this brother as she is with the older one.

We move to her home to flesh out the family and living situation. We see a large family eating outside, but they are not all biologically related. Her mother is there; the young woman describes her as a "good person, very fat." Lots of little kids are running around, and she explains that her father has children by multiple women. Although he is there, she does not feel particularly close to him.

There are a number of small residences clustered close to each other. The structures are not strongly constructed, and they're not used much except sometimes to sleep and to store things. There is, however, a strong wooden platform outdoors that is used all the time. The climate is tropical. The young woman observes that "you can just keep walking and walking" along the beach. Clearly we are in a Polynesian setting before modern civilization hit.

As we investigate family relations more closely, she identifies that she has an older brother who has his own family now. She also had a sister who was close in age but died a while ago. She has warm memories of her sister. They slept together, worked together, would sit together when they ate. "We would walk around to escape work and the others," she shared in amusement. "She suddenly got sick; I didn't see her die. They wrapped her body up. But it was OK; I told her everything, so there was nothing left to say," she adds matter-of-factly. When I ask Ruth to see if she recognizes that sister as someone she knows in her current lifetime, wondering if this might be Susie, she identifies her instead as another of her daughters.

"I sit with my mom," she continues. "Everyone is so sad. We burned the body, made food, cried. Death is just the way it is. It is part of our beliefs."

We move forward to the next major event in that lifetime. Her father is gone. "He left with some others and never came back," she says. "It's not really different. My brothers are still here. My mom doesn't really care; she didn't like him much."

As we move forward, the young woman is now in her thirties. She has no children, never having paired up with a man. She lives with her mother and is busy helping with the others' children. Her mom is older, but still round and happy. It is now that we identify the mother as Susie, Ruth's daughter who passed away.

Moving forward once again to the next significant event, her mother has died in her sleep. She is a bit surprised, as her mother wasn't all that old, but it felt like the right time nonetheless. "It was not a painful death," she recalls. "It was the right time for her. I was sleeping with her when she died.

"I'm bigger in body now. I take care of people. They come to be with me. I'm the 'auntie' and they talk to me. It's a good life. There are always so many kids! I don't do much work anymore. I'm pretty satisfied with this life."

I have her move to her last day of that lifetime. She's noticing that many things have changed. There are different children, and she is feeling very tired. She decides to sleep inside for a change. As she does so, she begins to dream that she can't breathe, and she passes over in her sleep: "Everyone's asleep. I just walk away from myself— down by the water, I just keep going." She finds herself moving to a place of quiet and pleasant color where she "feels good, alone but not alone."

As we process the lifetime, Ruth observes that the family was the key dimension: "Having everyone as one big family was very good; we were very fortunate to have that. It was a different kind of love— bigger. My family is small this lifetime; everyone is separate. I keep trying to bring them together, to make a big family, but people are too afraid to share their lives the way we did." She relates her sadness about this.

Acceptance of life and death is nonetheless the biggest lesson:

this is a fact, the way life is. As we pull in spiritual guidance from a higher plane, Ruth hears this message: "Susie just had to go; it's not so personal. The truth is you can't see her now, but that's all." She is also reminded that "there's no shortcut with the grieving process; it's how you learn to let go." An interesting observation is also given about the size of one's family. "Before there were so many, and now there is only one to take care of, but it's the same. One person can be your whole family, represent all those people. Size and volume do not matter." We clarify that the one person to take care of now is actually her youngest child, who still needs a mother's active involvement.

The session closes with Ruth receiving an image of three women in pale yellow dresses. They are looking in a drawer; it contains three marbles and something else: sorrow. Ruth identifies the red marble as her daughter Susie. And she is told, "Close the drawer; it's time." We finish the session by pulling in healing light energy.

———

It may seem rather coldhearted to tell a grieving mother not to take her daughter's death so personally. Or that it's time for her to close the drawer on her sorrow and move on. But remember, this advice was coming from Ruth herself—giving information and guidance from one part of herself to the part that was stuck in sorrow and grief. On some level we have all our answers within, and this must have been what Ruth needed to hear. The entire culture of this Polynesian lifetime seemed to have an attitude toward life and death that was well balanced. There was room to be sad and say good-bye to the loved one, but it also held an underlying philosophy that death was a very natural part of life and that life was meant to be lived by those still alive. This was a very important worldview for Ruth to experience and start to integrate into her current perspective.

It was wonderfully reassuring to have Susie show up, not as the sister who died, but as the large, jolly mother who lived a full and predominantly happy life surrounded by loving children and family. And instead, the beloved sister who died in the former lifetime is showing up as another daughter now. Each had chosen a position where they and Ruth could work through the loss of the other in this triangle of women. This was the three marbles in Ruth's parting imagery, no doubt.

ESSENTIAL TRUTHS UNCOVERED

* Accepting death as a natural part of life, knowing our loved ones carry on.
* Embracing grief as a necessary step in letting go.
* Creating family from who's available. It's the quality of relating, not the quantity of family members that counts.

EXPANDING YOUR PERSPECTIVE

Take a few moments to consider your attitude toward death, particularly your own death. Is it something you would rather not think about? Is it something you actually fear? Do you believe you will be returning to your source, a much better place, or going to an eternal reward? Does this make it something you look forward to?

Now think about the important people in your life who have died. Do you still feel a connection to them? How different would you feel if you knew you had been with them in many lifetimes in the past and that you will be together again in the future? You can cultivate a non-physical relationship with deceased loved ones: Go to that relaxing, private space and once again focus your attention inward. Imagine the beautiful bright light in front of you that emanates a wonderful feeling of deep peace and joy and divine love. In this light, the face of your loved one begins to take shape. Allow yourself to recall how you used to feel in this person's presence. Allow that feeling and the sense of connection between the two of you to expand. What would you like to say to this person? What does this person have to say to you? Enjoy being in each other's presence. Know that the connections of love between us do not die with the death of the physical body. How can a connection with those who have passed help you to more fully embrace your life now.

CHAPTER 17

When Our Bodies Carry Our Past

SOME OF THE MOST curious stories, in my mind, are those that arise from clients who want to investigate past life origins of physical symptoms in their current lives. It's intriguing how our physical bodies can either replay or carry vestiges of trauma from prior lifetimes. In addition, many times a condition will arise in the current life somewhere near the age at which the trauma occurred in the past life. How does all this work? Some practitioners theorize that on a metaphysical level our bodies are actually a combination of discrete yet interrelated energy systems: a physical energy body, an emotional energy body, a mental energy body, and a spiritual energy body. We can carry energy from one lifetime to another on any or all of these levels, and via this mechanism prior issues can reemerge in our current lives.

Of course, a physical symptom that relates to a prior life trauma typically will not occur in isolation; it will usually be accompanied by an emotional carryover (a phobia, perhaps) or beliefs about life or oneself (the mental energy body coming into play). So even though it's a little artificial to categorize clients' experiences according to one particular component, nonetheless many people come in with their predominant complaint being a physical ailment. On occasion, finding a past life link can eliminate or at least improve the problem (as was demonstrated in my own story about my feet in Chapter 1), but more often it provides understanding and loosens energy that may relate to other areas of the incident in question. And this can help alleviate the physical symptoms over time.

Some of the many physical symptoms that clients have investigated in regression, and the associated prior life experiences, are described below. This doesn't imply that everyone with that particular symptom will have the same cause, but it provides some ideas to consider.

Allergies and Asthma

One client had been plagued with allergies and asthma since adolescence. She was rarely able to breathe through her nose. In regression, she visited a lifetime as a man who was moved to help his neighbors who fell sick. In so doing, he wore himself ragged and became sick himself. Unfortunately, the local priests accused him of heretical healing practices and he was thrown in a dungeon, which made his condition worse. He found it extremely difficult to breathe and eventually died in the dungeon.

This client also shared that she suffered from diabetes but found it challenging to eat correctly. One of her lessons from this regression was she must help herself before helping others. She understood this to mean that she needed to address her diabetes before she could pursue her current business idea of opening a healing center so as not to repeat the mistakes of the prior personality.

Canker Sores

A man in his early forties consulted me about his recurring canker sores. This was one of the more unusual requests I've had about physical symptoms, and the resulting past life was surprising. He uncovered a lifetime as an orphaned Chinese girl who grew up in a brothel and eventually became a prostitute. There were many occasions when she was very poorly treated by men, including a beating by her male handler that injured her face all around her mouth. It was a short, unhappy life.

The client observed at the end of the session that this prior life had changed his attitude toward gender-related issues. He saw how negative men's behavior could be toward women and was determined to act differently in this lifetime.

Insomnia and ADHD

A twenty-year-old student came to see me about her insomnia, claiming that four hours of sleep a night was a great night for her. She had recurring nightmares that she was about to die, and traced this back to a young age. We uncovered a lifetime in France in the late 1300s when, as the daughter of a prominent political figure, she was expected to stay indoors to protect her complexion and follow only approved, ladylike pursuits. She was eventually married off to an older man who had similar requirements of her. In fact, he placed a guard on her during his frequent absences to make sure she didn't disobey his commands. This guard eventually became physically abusive, claiming she needed to learn her place.

The young woman became terrified of falling asleep, fearing either she would be attacked or that she would miss an opportunity to escape. She felt like a prisoner in her private room. Eventually, in a struggle she fell out a window to her death. In addition to the obvious link to the client's sleeping issues, this lifetime of being boxed up also connected to her ADHD (attention deficit hyperactivity disorder).

Restless Leg Syndrome

A somewhat similar issue arose for a woman who wished to investigate the origins of her restless legs. She described her feelings as "I can't be tied down, confined, or sit still." She found a prior life in the early 1900s when, as an older woman, her younger husband wished to be rid of her so he could pursue another love interest. He arranged for her to be hospitalized in a mental ward where she was tied down to the bed so she could hardly move. This went on for some time before she was released. The client reported that, even in her current life, a sense of freedom and self-determination was key.

Seizure Disorder and Obesity

The commitment of a wife to a mental ward came up again with a client who had suffered from occasional seizures since childhood. Although not epileptic, she was on seizure medication to control her symptoms. She went to a prior life in the 1950s where her husband, unable to divorce her and wanting control of the children, committed her to a mental institution where she was given repeated shock treatments. This same prior life also linked to her current obesity: the prior personality's parents had used withholding food as a method of punishment, and she herself would refuse to eat while in the mental hospital. In a sense, the client was overeating now to make up for all that deprivation.

Heart Palpitations/Irritable Bowel Syndrome

A professional woman wanted to track the source of her heart palpitations. She went to a lifetime in the British Isles in the 1400s. As a young man in his twenties, he lost his life from a sword through the chest in a skirmish with a neighboring clan.

Similarly, a client suffering for many years with irritable bowel syndrome discovered a prior life in which he was killed by a spear that was run through his gut from back to front. In both cases the clients' bodies were holding on to the physical trauma in the same location as the prior lifetime.

Metastasized Cancer

A female client in her late thirties had undergone treatment for cancer for the past three years. It had metastasized to many parts of her body, but by the time she saw me she had been cancer-free for seven months. She went to a lifetime as a soldier in World War II. His entire right side was blown away in an explosion and he died instantly. It seems the cancer was reflecting the massive trauma to the soldier's body. The client was advised by her guidance to live fully and enjoy life while she could. She was also advised that forgiveness of herself for any misdeeds, even those unconsciously carried from prior lifetimes, would be important for her continued health.

Fibromyalgia

A client in her mid-fifties had been diagnosed over twenty years earlier with fibromyalgia, a chronic disorder characterized by widespread pain throughout the body. In session, she got information on a number of lifetimes with physical trauma: as an Italian immigrant in Brooklyn, New York, who died from tuberculosis; as a Georgia coal miner who died quite young from black lung disease; as a young girl in the time of the Renaissance who lost the use of her legs when she was overrun by an oxcart; and as a young boy who survived polio but was crippled for life. Her body was apparently hanging on to the vestiges of pain from these incidents.

Foot, Ankle, and Back Pain

A client in her early fifties had chronic problems with pain in her feet, her back, and one of her ankles. The doctors couldn't really point to a specific cause. In her regression, she went to a lifetime as a young teenager. He went out exploring in the woods on his own and decided to investigate a crevice in a large rock. In the darkness inside, he fell and got trapped by his foot and hips. He had wrenched his ankle and was stuck in a very uncomfortable position that stressed his back. No one knew where he had gone, and he was unable to extricate himself. He died full of fear and feelings of guilt that he would not be around to help his mother and young sister.

It's not uncommon for intense feelings at the time of death to cause physical symptoms to carry over into another lifetime. As to why some people experience this and others don't seem to, that remains an area that warrants further study. The next three chapters look closely at some of the more dramatic stories of clients presenting with physical symptoms. Keep an eye out for other aspects, such as relationship issues or belief systems, that also crop up in these stories. As shown in most of the summaries above, the physical symptoms rarely occur in isolation.

EXPANDING YOUR PERSPECTIVE

Do a personal survey focused on your physical body. Do you have a chronic physical ailment that doesn't respond well to treatment or that the doctors just can't figure out? Do you find that a certain part of your body keeps giving you trouble? At what age did the complaint arise? What else was going on in your life at the time? Is there a particular way that you would describe the condition, such as "It's like a huge weight is on my chest" or "It feels like a knife in my back"? These analogies can be surprising clues to past life connections to current physical symptoms.

See if you can set up a dialogue with the troubled part of your body. It's helpful to actually write out a conversation in your journal between the two of you: Ask your body part what it wants to tell you. Actually write the question and then write out whatever answer pops into your mind. Ask it what it needs, what it wants, what it represents. Is "a pain in the neck" a perfect metaphor for something going on in your life right now? What would you need to do in the rest of your life to give that neck some relief? How is that painful neck preventing you from achieving fulfillment and purpose?

CHAPTER 18

No Way I'm a Nazi!

I HAD BEEN SEEING Peter for a number of years in a conventional counseling capacity, as a result of a serious fall that left him disabled and unable to work. My involvement centered on managing the emotional aspects of the chronic pain he suffered, as well as redefining his self-concept and sense of worth now that he could no longer be the active, capable man that he was used to being.

Peter and his wife had been unable to have children of their own, and they had been in the process of looking into adopting a child when the injury occurred. Peter's medical challenges and the severe drop in income put an end to that dream, which was a significant loss for the couple.

Getting insurance coverage for his injuries was an ongoing battle. Having come from a conservative background with an autocratic father who demanded respect for authority, Peter was now finding himself questioning authority at every turn, be it his former employer, attorneys, judges, doctors, or the entire system.

At one point Peter and I discussed the idea that it is not unusual for an individual to experience accidents or injuries that mirror an injury from a prior lifetime. We decided to try a past life regression, partially for the sake of curiosity but mainly in an attempt to derive some meaning out of what had happened to him. Maybe we would find an experience from a prior lifetime that was reflected in his current injury and the "war" that he felt he was waging with workers' compensation. Peter was not at the time a firm believer, but he was open to the possibility of prior lifetimes; he had a Mormon upbringing and knew that the belief in prior lifetimes had been a tenet of the early Mormon principles, even though it was not officially embraced now. His regression turned out to be one of the most memorable that I have experienced, largely because of the reaction he had to what he discovered.

———

"I'm in an aircraft—a military aircraft. I'm the navigator. We're losing altitude! Enemy aircraft shot out our engines—we're going down!" The regression begins at a moment of high drama and danger.

I relieve the intensity by stepping back to get some background and framework before allowing this dramatic scene to progress. We learn that his name is Daniel, and he was born in Omaha, Nebraska. He is about nineteen years old and has been in the war for a year. This is his first live run, however, and he's very nervous about it. They are flying over French farmland and have no communication with the ground.

"Where did you take off from?" I ask. I have a sneaking suspicion that there's a twist to this story.

"We took off from . . . Germany? I'm German! We're going to England on a bombing run!" Peter's current personality emerges with this realization even as he remains in his hypnotic state. He is absolutely flabbergasted and very upset that he is on the other side of the World War II conflict. This is not consistent with his current values and worldview. "I can't be a Nazi!" he protests.

We investigate how this came about, since he presumably is from Nebraska. His parents, immigrants to the United States from Germany, returned to their homeland with Daniel prior to the outbreak of the Second World War. Daniel was born in America and spoke

English up to the age of fourteen. "I had a lot of problems with school in Germany," he remembers.

"I enlisted in the German army because I had to. I'm a German citizen." We discover that, although only eighteen years old, he is already married. He sees the image of a young woman wearing a sleeveless dress with a blue flowered print. "She's small for her age, childlike," he observes. The marriage is not of his choosing but rather was arranged to comply with government directives. The powers that be want their fighting men to have wives and families to protect and fight for. "I don't really know her, and she doesn't like me; I'm not her ideal husband. We were only married six months before I left." By this time, however, as he goes off to war, Daniel reports having a sense of pride that he's living up to what is expected of him.

We now return to the dramatic opening scene. The engines are screaming as the wind spins the props. The plane is going down, but Daniel can't bail out. His position in the navigator's seat prevents that from even being a possibility. He's crammed into a small cubicle filled with instruments. It's dark and very cold.

"I have no control over the plane . . . I have to release myself to my fate . . . I know I'm going to die . . . I think of my father and my mother . . . I'm making my peace with it. But I feel like I've failed again." I probe to learn more about these feelings of failure. Daniel says he failed as a husband but particularly as a son. His father did not want him to enlist. "He generally scares me," Daniel says of his father. "He controls everything; he has authority, position. He wears a suit all the time. I failed him."

He hears the crunch of metal, the explosion of heat, sees flashing light, then blackness. As Daniel's body dies, his awareness floats up and he is able to look down on the mangled and burned plane. He can see body parts strewn around; there were a number of men still on board. His own body was thrown against the instrument panel.

The blackness grows, like a vacuum. He describes having some kind of awareness, but he senses and feels nothing, "like oblivion. It's scary, but it's not. Only if I think about it."

As we begin to process this death, Peter finds a connection to the sense of failure he felt. "We were made to feel that a lot depended upon our success," he explains. "But we failed. That's why I enlisted in the military in this [Peter's current] life; I had to complete my mission!" Peter explains that he enlisted in the U.S. Army Aviation Corps during the Vietnam War. He had wanted to be a pilot but was tested and found to have a very high aptitude for being a mechanic, so that became his role.

Suddenly, Peter has another intense memory. He is a passenger in a military aircraft flying over the jungle canopy in Vietnam. The pilot is having some fun, buzzing the treetops, but Peter is thrown into a panic. "We're too close! We're going to crash!" he cries. With this, he snaps out of his hypnotic state. His fear is just too intense.

Peter and I discuss the event in Vietnam. Although he hasn't thought about it for years, he confirms that this did indeed happen. A number of them were flying in a plane, and the pilot flew down close to the canopy. Peter panicked. It was quite out of character for him to react in such a manner, and he didn't understand it. He knew the plane was not out of control and they weren't really in danger, but it set off an unreasonable fear that he was unable to control.

Surprisingly, however, Peter does not remember anything else from the earlier part of the regression. I realize that finding himself as a Nazi is so ego dissonant for Peter that his psyche is protecting him from this conscious knowledge for a while. Since we have an ongoing relationship, we agree to give it a few days and see what he remembers before he listens to the recording of the session.

———

Sure enough, when Peter returned for our regularly scheduled counseling session, he reported experiencing flashbacks from the session as well as from the lifetime itself. He had a flood of images and insights, and he was still quite taken aback at the realization that he had been part of the German army. He remembered his wife's name to be Francesca. "She had blond hair and was disgusted with me. She was angry because she had not gotten pregnant and that was our duty according to the state." This was part of his feelings of failure as a husband: he had not fathered a child before his death. He noted the continued theme in his current lifetime of him and his wife being unable to have children.

Peter realized that although he did not know any German in his current life, during the regression he was thinking in German and a number of German words for everyday items were occurring to him spontaneously. He also experienced physical recall of the smells in the plane, the heat of the tubes from the instrument panel, and the utter coldness of the surrounding air.

We marveled at how falling from a considerable height and the major physical damage to many parts of his body in his current life reflected the experience of the plane crash in the prior lifetime. Fortunately, he survived it this time. Even more impactful for Peter, however, seemed to be the fact that he felt this prior life experience was what had compelled his behavior in many ways in his current life.

Up until his work injury, Peter described himself as being "like a conscript, following the party line." He had accepted that those with authority knew what they were doing. His job was to understand and execute their directives. One of his biggest realizations after his accident was to see that the system wasn't looking out for him after all. Being in a situation of powerlessness, having no control over his own life—as our young Nazi, Daniel, experienced in the plane going down—was remarkably similar to how Peter now felt in his struggle to get benefits.

For some months after the regression, we continued to integrate this experience into a greater sense of who he now was. It took Peter a while to make peace with his new role in questioning authority and looking out for his own interests. Although the regression could not heal his many injuries, it helped give him a structure in which to understand the lessons inherent in the experience for him.

Peter's story is a great illustration of the role that reincarnation plays as "the great equalizer." No matter what our current situation, beliefs, ethnic origin, or gender, we have undoubtedly been on the other side of that equation at some point along the way. In doing past life work, we actually get a sense of what the other side's experience is truly like. We find ourselves living in many different parts of the world, being ardent followers of very different religions, holding different political, social, and moral values. We may go from penniless beggar to wealthy aristocrat; from powerful man to abused woman; from Christian to Muslim; from monk to centurion. And in each life experience, our religion, our culture, and our beliefs are what make us who we are and determine many of our actions and decisions. Thus, Peter, who would never dream in this life of playing a role in the atrocities perpetrated by Hitler, finds himself as a Nazi airman in World War II. It does not excuse actions we find untenable, but it certainly helps us compassionately understand and perhaps relate to the diversity of thought, feeling, and experience in this world.

ESSENTIAL TRUTHS UNCOVERED

* Making your own decisions instead of following the "party line."
* Questioning authority when your interests are at stake.
* Detaching self-esteem from your performance or role in society.
* Experiencing the worldview of someone with very dissimilar beliefs. This instills humility and compassion.

EXPANDING YOUR PERSPECTIVE

How would an experience like this impact you? What would it be like to realize that a prior personality had been the very thing that you find untenable now? How would you reconcile yourself to that? What would you learn from it? Might it make you a more understanding and compassionate person toward others? Allow some time to ponder this more deeply.

CHAPTER 19

Speaking Your Truth

SOMETIMES CLIENTS come to me wanting to pursue lifetimes that they were told about by a psychic or medium. They want to learn more details and have a direct experience with the memories of that past life. It is typically a much more vivid and impactful experience to recall and relive your own past life rather than just being told about it from a third party. The specifics of the lifetime are usually fleshed out in clearer detail, the story can be followed from beginning to end to see how and why situations developed, and the emotional impact is readily apparent and available to be worked through. However, I never mind getting a jump start from a reputable psychic indicating what direction in our regression work might be most helpful to the client. I'm comfortable knowing that if for some reason the psychic's information is incorrect, then the client will go to a different, valid lifetime.

Barbara had been told about two prior lifetimes in a reading by an energy healer. As I looked over her client information form, I was surprised to learn she was a Christian minister. I just didn't expect a conventional religious professional to be consulting energy healers and past life therapists. So much for my preconceived notions! Barbara wanted to delve deeper into the lifetimes and their impact on her life now. The first life was as a pioneer woman in a Mormon settlement—a plural wife who was outspoken and was subsequently thrown out, leaving behind two sons. The other lifetime was very brief: a three-year-old child in Ireland who died of exposure after her parents died in a famine. We agreed to focus on the Mormon lifetime, since it seemed there would be rich material to work with.

Before starting the regression, Barbara shared that she considered herself to have abandonment and control issues, which she attributed to long hospital stays and numerous reconstructive surgeries for a cleft palate as a child. She mentioned having a particular sensitivity to her environment being either too hot or too cold. As we launched into the regression, I had no idea how strongly the cleft palate in this lifetime was going to reflect issues from the past.

———

Barbara drops quickly into a deeply relaxed state. As I direct her to her lifetime as a Mormon plural wife, her first image is of dry ground under her feet. She is wearing a long skirt that nearly brushes the ground and is made of a rough, brownish, undyed cotton. On her upper torso she wears a long-sleeved white blouse that buttons down the front and at the wrists. Her hair is pulled back into a bun. She describes her hair color as a "light dirty blond" and says she's not wearing a cap or bonnet. She has light-blue eyes and a narrow face, and feels she is in her early twenties.

The young woman is overcome with a deep feeling of sadness. "I feel like I'm stuck. I want to stop pretending, but I can't," she laments. I ask her what it is that she is pretending about. "I pretend to be happy doing what I've been told is the woman's role," she says, "but it's not enough." She's sad because she knows the other women are lying too.

"So what is the woman's role here?" I ask her.

"You can't ask questions," she says. "You can't read what you want to"—adding that, yes, indeed, she does know how to read. "I think the men are afraid of me," she reflects, "because I question. I know I'm smarter than my husband, but he doesn't see it."

I ask her to bring an image of her husband forward and describe him. He's middle-aged, of average height, and "plain" in her words. She describes his personality as "boring," and she mentions that she doesn't look at him much. He's a farmer, and he's strong, but "he doesn't like to think; he likes to do. He likes rules and he likes his family to obey. When we were first married, I asked questions, but he shot me down," she says, sighing. The look on his face indicated to her that he was afraid of her intelligence.

I ask her to go back to the time of their wedding, when she was about sixteen. "I was too young to think of anything but happiness," she reflects. "My parents were happy even though my mother was not a plural wife. We came to the community when I was a schoolgirl." The community consists of multiple families, all of them practicing plural marriage, or polygamy. It's a settlement but not quite a city yet.

I direct her to her home. It's a wooden house with a number of rooms and stairs just inside the front door. A family meal is often a good place to see the family members and the dynamics of their relationships, so I ask her to go to the time of their last family meal. The eating room contains one long table. Her husband is at the head of the table and is talking to the eldest son, who's about twelve. "He's not mine," she says. "My sons are with me: John, who's six, and David, who's three." She sees two other wives and their children, some of them babies. The first wife comes into focus as a very important figure.

"She has a lined face, dark hair that's partly gray; she's about the age of my husband," the young woman says. I probe about her relationship with the first wife. "She doesn't like me; she thinks I'm dangerous, but she has not been a happy woman since childhood. She's conflicted because she thinks she should be happy, but she's bitter." Apparently the first wife is angry about having to share her husband with sister wives. Since she has grown up within the plural marriage community and has never known anything else, she thinks there must be something wrong within herself.

"And I'm confused," our young woman says. "I expected to be

mentored, have her help me figure out about plural marriage, help me find peace and learn how to deal with our husband—but she doesn't know, either!" She begins to cry. "Everyone is so sad! He's not happy, either, except when he's in the field or teaching his sons— and when the kids are born. I don't think he understands anything else!"

The second wife, who has a couple of daughters, is "mousy, almost not there. She wants to hide," according to our young woman. "I'm the third wife. I'm on my own; my parents are elsewhere. They married me off and then moved." It sounds extremely lonely for her. "I write to my mom," she says with longing.

I ask her what, if anything, brings her some pleasure in this life. "I tell the kids stories at bedtime." She smiles. "The things I imagine in my head."

Feeling that we have sufficient background now, I ask her to move forward to a significant event when something important occurs. She's being pulled by the wrist by the first wife: "I said something to her." All three wives are in the house together. "I asked why she didn't tell us the truth about her not wanting us, the other wives. She knew what plural marriage was like and what our husband was like. She knew what we were getting into, but I didn't. She didn't share about only doing housework, not being able to think or read or meet anyone or go anywhere! She was afraid to tell the truth!"

The first wife slaps her for her insolence and then grabs her by the wrist. "She's afraid I'll never shut up," she says. "It's not safe to question. I'm threatening her existence and making her think about things." The first wife drags her down the stairs while the second wife hides in her room. Our young woman feels confused, alarmed, and really angry that the first wife won't admit to the truth.

The first wife pulls her out to the field to their husband. She's sick of her questioning and rebelliousness.

"If she's questioning 'the Principle' [plural marriage], then she must not be trustworthy; she'll contaminate the children!" the first wife asserts to their husband. He's angry that his work has been in-terrupted and wants to be left alone.

"He's mad I'm causing trouble again," our third wife observes. He tries to extract a promise from her that she will change her ways, but she knows she can't. "I won't promise. I want to go back to my parents if he doesn't want me there." She can tell he's conflicted; he wants her gone, but he's worried about the humiliation he would suffer within the community.

"Let me take the boys and go to my parents," she pleads. "Send me back." This enrages him. "The boys aren't yours to take," he insists. "If you want out, you can leave. Run away. But I won't help you. You have to promise to be obedient or leave now!"

The third wife gives in. She says she will be obedient. She can't leave her sons. "I'll do whatever you want," she says in defeat.

But the first wife refuses to buy it. "She'll turn the boys against you," she warns their husband. "I can't watch her all the time! I will tell the elders you knew she made a false promise and let her stay. She has to go!" The first wife is filled with vengeance.

The young woman wants to go back into the house. "They can't make me leave them! It's too overwhelming. I can't leave them; they won't understand!" she says, referring to her young boys. But the first wife is unrelenting. She has the husband take the third wife in a buggy to the edge of town, where he drops her off unceremoniously.

"Go home to your parents. Don't ever come back" are his final words to her.

"I'm going to pray and get to my parents," she says desperately. "I don't know how. I'm hoping that someone will help me. I'm not even sure how to get to them," she laments. "It's too far to walk."

Yet that is what she does, for at least a couple of days. She does have some water, but she becomes lost in her wandering and reaches exhaustion. *I have to get to my parents,* she thinks frantically. *They'll help me. I have to get my boys. I don't know what they've been told. They'll be so scared and sad.*

We move to the conclusion of this event. She finds herself curled up on the ground, suffering abdominal cramping and bleeding. She's having a miscarriage. "They must not have known yet that I was pregnant," she says. "He wouldn't have sent me away." The bleeding won't stop, and she soon moves to her death. Her final thoughts are of her two sons: "I let them down. They'll think I left them, they [the other family members] will tell them horrible things about me and raise them in that unhappy place. No one knows where I am—they won't find me for weeks! My husband will say I ran away and abandoned them."

As we process this lifetime after the death and look at the parallels between that lifetime and her current life, Barbara draws a number of conclusions. "Silence is painful" is a key observation. She also acknowledges just how painful it is to feel that you have let your children down. She realizes that although John, the older son, does not seem familiar to her in her current life, the younger son, David, does. She believes he is one of her daughters in her current life, an opportunity to make up for her absence from her child's life at such a young age in the prior lifetime.

In that earlier life, Barbara placed a very high value on telling the truth and using her intelligence to question the status quo, even at great cost. "Not everyone tells the truth about themselves or what they see, however," she acknowledges, noting that her current mother was raised in a family where the truth was not safe: her reports of abuse were not believed. Her mother married for safety rather than love and lived in painful silence. Barbara points out that she can always speak the truth herself now, and her current family tells the truth to each other. She values this very much. She also says that she still delights in telling her children stories from her imagination.

As we finish our processing and access higher guidance, Barbara is told that the older son, John, knew that the first wife was lying about the facts surrounding his mother's departure. When he was older, John sought out the grandparents, who discerned the truth about the situation. John learned about his mother and who she really was from his grandmother. David, the younger child, she is told, is receiving his healing through their relationship in the current lifetime.

———

So what about the cleft palate that she was born with in this lifetime, and why do I include this as a story about physical symptoms? Indeed, Barbara's story demonstrates a number of dynamics, as many regressions do. This story certainly illustrates the continuation of family connections across lifetimes. Also, with what the medium had told Barbara about the short life in Ireland, where she died from exposure after being orphaned, and this Mormon lifetime, in which she also was abandoned and died exposed to the elements, it is clear that her abandonment and environmental control issues, although exacerbated by childhood trauma in the hospital, may also have been carried over from prior life experiences. Control issues in general were prevalent in the Mormon lifetime, and being controlled or told who to be by another would certainly be a hot button for her.

But the physical parallel with the cleft palate seemed most dramatic to me, even though that was not what Barbara was planning to investigate with the past life session. In fact, she did not make the connection herself until I pointed it out. The key theme we uncovered was the ability to speak one's truth. Doing so cost her not only her family but her very life as a Mormon plural wife. She arrived in this lifetime with a cleft palate that required numerous painful surgeries just in order for her to speak clearly. She could have been very self-conscious about speaking and have shied away from expressing herself her entire life. Instead, she overcame the obstacles, painful though the process was, and actually became a preacher whose life's work is sharing "the Word." And she created a family culture in which telling the truth was highly valued. What a triumphant turnaround! I would say that was one lesson well integrated and mastered.

ESSENTIAL TRUTHS UNCOVERED

* Recognizing the importance of speaking your truth.
* Breaking free from the oppression of rigid gender roles.
* Experiencing family connections across lifetimes.

EXPANDING YOUR PERSPECTIVE

Most of us have had lifetimes in which speaking our truth led to dire consequences. After all, other than the Renaissance, human history is not noted for vast periods of open-minded tolerance for people who challenged the conventional way of doing things. Maybe that's one of the reasons surveys show that public speaking is the number one fear that people have.

How would you assess your ability and commitment to speaking your truth in your current life? Is it an issue for you, or something you do quite naturally? Are there some people or situations that make it more difficult for you? How can you safely expand your sense that you can speak your truth and be heard and accepted? How would this impact your belief that you can manifest what you want in your life?

CHAPTER 20

A Dire Pregnancy

I RECEIVED AN E-MAIL from a young woman saying she and a dear childhood friend were going to be meeting up in California and they both were interested in having a regression session. Fun thing to do on your vacation! Actually, it's not that unusual a request. I've had clients vacationing from as far away as India, Belgium, South America, and New Zealand come to see me during their travels, as well as people from all across the United States. Savannah was a delightful young professional woman in her early thirties who worked in real estate. Other than that, I knew very little about her. Her objective for the regression was mainly for exploration, so our entry point was whatever lifetime would be most significant for her to see at that time.

Savannah's first impression is of black, flat shoes, made of some lightweight material other than leather. White socks are worn on the feet, and the shoes are a slip-in style. She identifies herself in a female body, petite, and about twenty years old. She wears simple, black three-quarter-length trousers made of a lightweight, smooth, cotton-like material. On her upper body, she is adorned in a bright turquoise top with long, wide sleeves, of a satiny texture, and with some kind of prominent illustrations on it. She describes herself as

Asian in features and coloring, with long black hair pulled back. At this point, she is not sure if she is Chinese or Japanese.

We turn our attention to her surroundings. She is in a busy outdoor marketplace. She has come there alone, but there are many people milling around. There are many stalls where produce, meats, and various other food and farm products are being sold. I ask if she is there to buy or sell, and her surprising response is "Someone is being killed." She doesn't really want to see it, but it's what everyone does around her. They're beheading a man for stealing. "He looks at me, even though I don't know him. I'd like to stop it but don't know how. I have no control or influence. I feel helpless." It is a dramatic and upsetting scene, very early in the regression.

I have her turn her attention to her home so we can get a little more grounding in this lifetime. She lives in a bamboo hut on one of the streets in the town. When I ask who else lives there with her, she identifies a number of children, all younger brothers and sisters, except for one older brother. She describes her mother as a happy woman, with whom she has a good relationship, and identifies her as Savannah's mother in her current life. Her father is a fisherman who works hard and is quite distant; she doesn't feel much connection with him. However, Savannah is also able to identify him as her father in her current life. She describes her older brother as tall and strong, and he does some kind of work other than fishing. They have a good relationship; she describes them as being very close, and Savannah believes he is her cousin in the present.

The young woman lives with the family and appears fairly content with her life. She helps by earning money. I ask what kind of work she does. She sees herself wearing a big hat, working with others in a field, cultivating dry ground. Not easy work, but "I'm happy I have a job," she says. "I enjoy my friends at work."

I ask her to jump forward in that lifetime to a significant event. She is pregnant with her first child. However, she is unmarried, and this is a source of great shame. When I probe into the identity of the father, the news is even worse. It is her brother. "We love each other," she proclaims, and the sexual relationship has been going on for some time. "But we hid this; it is considered very bad!" Despite knowing that incest is taboo in their culture, they can't help themselves.

When he learns that she is pregnant, her brother convinces her to run away with him. They find an empty hut in the woods, close to a different village. They live as a couple but try to stay to themselves as much as possible. "I feel shame and guilt," she says. "But my brother wants to protect me."

When the baby comes, her brother tries to manage the delivery on his own. It is a difficult delivery; the baby is not able to move through the birth canal, and the young woman is in considerable pain. Her brother goes to get someone to help, but she dies before he returns. She feels a sense of surrender and calm at her death.

"My spirit tries to comfort him after my death," she observes. "He doesn't know I'm OK; I want him to know that. I stay with him a long time. He's really stuck. He kills himself eventually."

We move into healing work after viewing his death. "We're angry with each other," she notes. "He's angry because I left him. I'm angry because he should not have killed himself. We need to let go of each other."

I ask Savannah to bring forward a wise and loving being who can help her in working through this anger and conflict. "Why do we have to let go?" she asks her guidance. She is told, although it's not a require-ment, it would be good for each of them to learn to be alone. "You love each other unconditionally, no matter what you do," she is told. "It is easy; just let go of the past with each other. The past is not important."

In reviewing the lessons learned in that lifetime, Savannah has some interesting conclusions: Learn how to fully give love; learn how to follow your heart despite the cost or despite others trying to hold you back; learn about independence. These might not be the same conclusions another would draw from this experience, but she seems to have been able to release the negativity of the situation around the incest, the shame of the pregnancy, and their resulting deaths. However, it appears her body has still been holding on to something related to that experience. Savannah shares that, in her current life, she can't get pregnant. She and her husband have been trying unsuccessfully to have a child for some time. She draws a direct connection with the dire consequences of the pregnancy in the past.

———

This is another example of something totally unexpected coming up in a regression session. Both Savannah and I were quite surprised by the story that unfolded. At first, it seemed that the opening scene, when a man was being beheaded in the marketplace for stealing, might be of significance. Instead it turned out that that was just an anchoring event that brought her into the lifetime that she needed to see. Sometimes certain scenes or minor events within a prior life make an impression that we seem to carry with us that somehow are the linchpins that can pull us back into that particular life. It isn't always the pivotal event that we step into; at times that does happen, but it's usually just too sudden if it's a traumatic occurrence. For example, a different client came in to work on her chronic allergy and asthma problems—a feeling of not being able to breathe—and her immediate first impression was being strangled to death by an angry suitor. It was very sudden and very startling, and we had to do a lot of backtracking to calmly build back up to the event itself so the client could go through it without being traumatized again.

Savannah's case is also a good demonstration of the results of an open-ended "whatever is most significant for me to see" approach. Her higher self knew that she was in much turmoil about not being able to get pregnant, even though I had no idea that was an issue for her. So she went to a lifetime where the key issue was an incestuous pregnancy that had dire results all around—for mother, father, and baby. No one survived. We could see how carrying forward that kind of energy unknowingly could block the possibilities of pregnancy in the present.

When writing this chapter, I decided to see if I could contact Savannah, even though it had been seven years since we had worked together. I was able to communicate with her via e-mail, and here was her report:

> My husband and I have been blessed with a son. He is sixteen months old now and keeps us very busy. We needed the help of IVF [in vitro fertilization] to have him, but got lucky on our first try. I also managed to have a natural birth, although I remember thinking at the time it was a mistake. Ha ha . . . When I was younger I had always thought my life would be over when I had kids, but now having had one I realize my life has just begun.

Words to warm a therapist's heart.

ESSENTIAL TRUTHS UNCOVERED

* Giving love fully.
* Following your heart despite the cost.
* Forging your independent path in life.

EXPANDING YOUR PERSPECTIVE

What do you think about Savannah's conclusions drawn from this seemingly disastrous prior lifetime? Did they surprise you as they did me? This demonstrates how what appear to be negative experiences and situations may actually contain real gifts for us if we know how to look. Think about any seemingly negative events or circumstances in your current life. Keep your eyes open for the unexpected gifts these situations may bring. There are often rich opportunities within our most challenging experiences.

CHAPTER 21

Finding Higher Spiritual Guidance

ULTIMATELY, PAST LIFE regression work is an adventure into the spiritual aspects of our existence. Even though clients may come in seeking help with relationship issues, physical ailments, and emotional challenges, as they untangle these conundrums of daily life they also have the opportunity to get in touch with a deeper level of being. When clients move through the death experience in a prior lifetime, they realize that even as their bodies die, their awareness is ongoing. Existence does not end with the death of the physical body. What they see "on the other side" is profoundly reassuring, comforting, and full of an amazing sense of divine love. Many clients report the nonphysical state as a place of peace and bliss that they never want to leave.

Clients are also able to access a degree of wisdom that can be difficult to access on their own, unless they are master meditators. Even if all our answers are truly within, we often need facilitation to help unlock those answers for ourselves. Clients come in with all sorts of backgrounds in meditation and spiritual work, from those who have never tried to meditate to those who have done so consistently for three or more decades. It often doesn't seem to make a difference for the degree of spiritual wisdom and guidance they are able to tap into. Every single regression has the chance of delivering some potent spiritual truths and guidance for the client.

I never know when some amazing spiritual content is going to crop up. At times clients can seem fairly naïve in the current life rather than deep or thoughtful, and their spiritual guidance brings in a powerful download of information. It keeps me on my toes, ready and waiting for the next gems coming from unlikely places. Ultimately, it demonstrates that we are all reflections of the divine, and as a result we can access untold levels of love and wisdom.

When consulting me, some clients go straight to the crux of the matter and come in with the specific intent of identifying that elusive life purpose for their current life or of boosting their movement along their spiritual development. These are always exciting sessions for me. I was particularly surprised many years ago when a swami (a trained Hindu spiritual teacher) from India asked to have a session. What would I be able to offer him that he had not already discovered in his spiritual work? The swami merely explained that he wanted to "explore the spiritual arena."

This spiritual teacher went to a lifetime in the early 1900s as a temple boy in India who was able to connect with the mysteriousness of life and the god force that exists in all forms. "Learn from everything," he was told, "the birds, the tortoise, the sunrise, the trees, the moon. God is teaching you through all these forces. God has no form, and all these forms." It seemed the temple boy found it easier to connect with the intensity of the god experience, but the swami was reassured that his current life was about sharing the light, teaching, and communicating. "The intensity of experience was greater then, but you were not communicating to others. Now it is less intense, but you are communicating."

Apparently the pendulum had swung a little too far, however. He was advised to work on deepening his experience in the here and now. "Don't get lost in only expressing; focus more on the experiencing now. Give time to it. Be open to the blessings of pure love and goodness." Even this spiritual teacher from India was able to connect with guidance beyond what he had been able to pull in for himself on his own. And it was a message that applies to most of us: Give time to it; focus on experiencing; be open to pure love.

Another surprising client was a woman who worked as a psychic and was able to channel information for others. She wished to gain greater focus on what she was meant to do with these abilities, and also to understand why her life had been so challenging in this lifetime. A prior life came through in which she had an agonizing death as an accused witch, which her spiritual guidance told her was necessary to learn compassion for others. The main focus of her session was a rich amount of higher guidance. She was told she had chosen extreme hardship this lifetime, to learn to let go, to clear karma from the past, and to achieve significant personal growth.

"This is very hard, and you must have a strong spiritual center; it is too upsetting if you are not connecting all the time," she was instructed. "Be as strong as an oak; drop your roots down. You can lose your leaves in the storm, but they grow back. You can help many people, but few can help you. You must recharge yourself through withdrawal, purification, connecting with God." The guidance and advice went on and on, touching on many aspects of her life. It was an inspiring session to be a part of, and by the end she was also pulling in advice and guidance for me.

Many times the guidance that comes through for a particular client has widespread applications for most of us. Here are some of my favorite gems of wisdom that have come through for clients while in that amazing interlife space between physical incarnations. I transcribed these close to their original forms, which involve some slang and less-than-perfect grammar, to keep the feel of the message and expression authentic while in a client session:

- It's so silly to worry about the small things in life, because when we die, we realize it's such a peaceful and comfortable place we're going to. The daily worries and head trips are all nonsense.

- Release judgments of yourself; things you do in your life are what you had to do; it's just what's in front of you. At the end, we all go to the same place. Do your best to take care of each other; give love to others. That's what's important in this life.

- It's just this place we spend time for a while. Share your truth with others; the only important things are compassion and love; we're all the same. If everyone understands that, the world becomes what it should be: a peaceful, loving place.

- We waste life by wanting what we don't have. Love others as they are. . . . See inside, beyond what they seem to be. Guide your love in the right direction, not just where it's easy.

- There is good reason we're not allowed to see what happens next. Life was meant to unfold—we're not meant to rush it, to force it. We have to let it happen. It's important to know you can trust what will happen, not be apprehensive. Release fear and anxiety—ride the wave; let it take you to shore. You can't always ride the crest; at times you tumble on the bottom, scraped, and bumped; hold on and you will get back to the surface, where you can enjoy the ride.

- Love your life, or change your life so you're happy. Take the thorns out of your feet, and do the dance without blaming others for your situation or unhappiness.

———

The next group of regression stories is from clients whose main quest in their sessions was to determine life purpose or promote spiritual growth, or where spiritual guidance played a particularly significant role.

EXPANDING YOUR PERSPECTIVE

Here is a technique you can use when the demands of the world seem to be crowding in on you and you would like to achieve more balance in your day. This practice, which I call "Empty and Full," was given to a client by her higher guidance during a session. I found it to be generally applicable and have suggested it to a number of other clients as well as having used it myself.

Take a few moments to meditate by focusing in your mind's eye on emptying your life from the noises and distractions of the world as you breathe out: EMPTY. Then focus on filling yourself with love and tranquillity as you breathe in: FULL.

Use this breathing technique as you do a number of rounds of slow, deep breaths. Follow the breath as it moves up through the central channel of the body, from base chakra to crown chakra as you breathe in, and then back down again as you breathe out. This can be very effective in moving you to a more peaceful state. Then you will be more able to address the needs of the moment with balance and consciousness.

CHAPTER 22

A Spanish Nobleman

IN THE LATTER stages of her work life, Denise had enjoyed a wide variety of careers. She had gone through a divorce a couple of years earlier, which spurred an increased interest in spirituality. Denise read widely and began to meditate and work with crystals and sound therapy, feeling she might be able to cultivate the ability to channel higher knowledge to help others. Her quest with past life work was to accelerate her spiritual path at this point in her life, and she was interested in seeing if she could get a clearer picture of the role she might play in what she called "lightwork service."

Denise had an impressive will and strong intuitive abilities. After having been a smoker for many years, she quit cold turkey using self-hypnosis. She had a specific spiritual guide named Gray Owl, an older Native American chief who would show up in her meditations, and she had received a number of visual images and scenes that she believed were from past lifetimes. These scenes included a young American soldier from the North in the Civil War who died from a bullet in the throat; a French scout in the French and Indian War in America's Colonial days; and the image of a Chinese woman wearing white makeup. It would be interesting to see if any of these lifetimes would show up or if something else altogether would come through.

Denise moves easily to a deep level of relaxation. Her first image is of tall black riding boots made of supple leather. Continuing up are black leggings, a black shirt of a soft material with a V-neck, and finally, a black cape. A jeweled scabbard carrying a sword hangs from a black belt. He is a fighting man: very strong, well trained, and about twenty years old. He describes himself as good-looking, with a sweet smile, blue eyes, a slight beard and mustache, and long black hair that hangs free. He cuts quite a dashing figure.

As we turn our attention to the surroundings, he finds himself indoors in his father's library. "There are too many books," he remarks. "My father's books. He loves reading, but it's not for me." The young man, whose name we learn is Roberto, lives in his father's house. He is alone in the library, waiting for his father.

When his father arrives, we take a moment to consider him. "He's way too fat; gone to hell, not fit," his son criticizes. He considers his father to be old, about sixty, with a gray beard. He wears an embroidered red vest with gold stitching. His shirt is brown, and he also sports leggings and boots. Over the top, he wears a long coat with a collar.

"I'm ashamed of him," Roberto comments. "He drinks too much. The property and land are going to hell. He never was a nice man. I'm better than him." He continues angrily, "I'm the heir. I've done so much for him, but it's not appreciated. I've protected him and his lies. He's a fake!" I ask about these lies and why he considers his father to be a fake. Roberto explains that his father invented stories of being famously heroic in battle, when he's never actually been in one. Apparently he has protected his father's image over the years by not exposing the truth.

As the meeting in the library proceeds, the young man observes that his father "is trying to make me feel small and ashamed, too—that there's no real meaning in fighting." Roberto is incensed: "To fight for a worthy cause has great honor! You must know how to fight and serve!" he insists. He shares that he has fought in many lands already.

Since his father has no experience or skill in battle, I wonder how

Roberto gained his fighting skills. He explains that he was trained by his uncles—of whom there are six—when he was quite young. It's time to place this lifetime in history, if possible, so I ask if he can identify a time and place. It is 1799 in Spain, around Barcelona. Roberto and his people have been fighting the Moors: "They stink," he sneers. "And their religion is false. I'm Catholic; I believe in the Virgin Mary." He states this as if nothing more need be explained about the righteousness of his stance.

Roberto is angry after the confrontation in the library with his father. (By the way, we identify the father as Denise's brother in her current life.) He goes to the stables and finds his favorite horse. It is a beautiful black stallion, and they are "as one" when he rides. He rides and rides until he no longer feels angry, and then pauses by a river on his own lands. Gypsies are there. *I think I'll scare them,* he considers. *What fun!* He rides at them, scattering them in all directions. "You thieves! Pigs! Even the little children are dirty," he says in disgust.

Later in the day he returns home, feeling quite hungry. The cook gives him bread and meat to eat and wine to drink. "I love this cook," he says warmly. "She's very fun, very kind to me." He describes her as gray-haired, fat, and happy, always singing and with a twinkle in her eyes. "She tells me I'm too wild; I need to take more care," he tells himself. "But I'm blessed! Nothing would happen to me. I was born with a veil over my face; it's a sign of luck." (This veil refers to a hood or caul that is the remnants of the amniotic sac left after birth, and for some cultures it was considered a very auspicious omen.)

I want to learn a little more about Roberto's family. He does not remember his mother, who died of an illness when he was young. He has a married sister in the next town whom he visits often. "She didn't want to marry, but our father forced her," he explains. "Now she is happy; she has a child." And he has twin siblings: a boy, Miguel, and a girl, Josephina. They are about twelve years old and have a different mother than he does, but that doesn't seem to make a difference. He loves them a lot and feels quite close to both of them.

"But I will never marry," he asserts. "It is best to be alone, to be free, not tied down. To do what I want—to fight, to ride. To be fancy-free is very important to me; I don't want ties." It's a little amusing from where I sit, as he has very strong emotional ties with his siblings, and family seems very important to him. And sure enough, when we move forward, we find him in a different frame of mind. "I'm older, more relaxed," he explains. "I own land and I'm a father. I'm married with four boys."

He describes his wife as very beautiful, with black hair and eyes. She is "tall and strong, with a proud chin. She is proud of our land, of our country, of me." He reflects on how he himself has changed. "I shepherd the land. I'm kinder; I don't chase Gypsies anymore. I like animals and I grow crops. The land is bountiful: the trees bear fruit; there are fish in the river. I've also learned that it's not wise to be proud as if I am superior to others and therefore that I need to kill them." His uncles are all still alive and are very rich from war booty. "They are proud men," he remarks. "I'm proud of them." Although his attitudes are evolving, pride obviously still holds a very significant place in his assessments. As you can see, he uses the word "proud" repeatedly in his descriptions.

As we move forward, Roberto suffers an illness that saps his strength. He receives a vision of the Virgin, who tells him he still has hate in his heart and that it is causing his heart to die. He needs to change: "The Virgin is very much in my heart," he asserts. "I always pray to her." Although he is a little weakened, he recovers sufficiently from the illness.

I ask Roberto to jump to the next significant event in his life. There has been a devastating house fire. A lantern fell over in the barn and ignited a blaze that spread and destroyed everything, even killing his wife. "I can't live without her," he laments. "My children are all gone and I'm very old, in my seventies." He prays to the Virgin to take him, feeling there is too much sadness to rebuild. Besides that, "Everyone's gone," he explains. "People went to a new land over the sea." Gossipy women come in from the village to gawk and offer some assistance, but they are no help. "It's time to go soon," he says.

"I love the land," he reflects. "It's good, fertile, warm; it's sensuous. The earth means so much to me. I have been a proud warrior; I've been brave; I've lived fully. There is nothing to be ashamed of. I resisted love, but it came to me anyway. I felt sad that my father couldn't help what he was. But my sister taught me a lesson about accepting your lot, and it can turn out."

We move to the moment of Roberto's death. He is sitting in a chair by a fire with his dog. His heart hurts, and he finds it hard to breathe. "I have to go slow," he says. "I'm very thin and bald. But I don't want to leave the land," he protests.

As he passes over, he exclaims: "I knew it! I see the Virgin and Jesus! He tells me I'm forgiven—for the pride, the hate, for killing so many people, for my lack of kindness to the Gypsies." He continues his initial observations upon his death. "There is so much love here . . . I didn't know how to love . . . They want me to go with them . . . I see my father . . . I see my whole life . . . Everyone is here! They're taking me to the land; it's OK. My horse is here too!"

There are many, many lessons for Roberto as he looks back upon the life just lived: Don't be so proud; don't feel that you're better; instead be humble. Don't kill. Be kinder; accept others. He experienced a life in which the land played an important role as a support and base. This was a life of strong religious faith, and Roberto is told that there is more than being brave; there is divine love. In fact, he is told, "Next time, focus on love and God."

As we draw parallels with Denise's current life, she sees the themes of forgiveness, love, spirituality, and kindness woven through both lifetimes. Distancing herself from family is an issue she identifies as one she is still working on. She also acknowledges that it's important for her to accept her body now as it is—certainly less magnificent than Roberto's in his prime. And she continues to have a great love of animals.

As we access higher guidance from the spiritual realm, Gray Owl appears, Denise's guide from her daily meditations. "Open your heart through service," she is told. "Help others—teach, talk, share your spiritual knowledge. Share what you know to be true." She is assured that she will gain in knowledge and wisdom as time goes on. "You are very protected," Gray Owl continues. "Many guides are helping you in meditation. In sleep, they are teaching you to go out of body; this just needs practice and faith. Grab a hand and let them pull you out," he instructs her. Denise shares that she has indeed been quite interested in astral projection, or sending her awareness out of her body to other parts of the world. It scares her a bit, feeling a little afraid she may not be able to come back from such nighttime wanderings. I suggest that before she goes to sleep, she invite her spiritual guides to help her with the process, releasing the earth, knowing she will safely return.

One of the things about this regression that was fun for me was the way that Denise completely stepped into the personality of Roberto. This can differ quite a bit from client to client. For some, it is more a reporting of what the other personality was thinking or feeling. In the case of clients like Denise, a therapist can reexperience what it would be like to be in the presence of the prior personality. Roberto comes through loud and clear with the pride in his voice as he talks about his battle skills and abilities. He doesn't hold back in expressing his strong attitudes and opinions of others. He calls the Gypsies dirty thieves and pigs; he is disgusted by how the Moors stink; and he is very forceful in his insistence on the rightness of his viewpoints. And it's very amusing to me, late in the session, when Roberto proclaims: "I need to go outside to relieve my bladder. Is this possible?" Instead, we paused, and Denise used the indoor restroom facilities before we finished the session.

I have had some other entertaining examples of a client really assuming a past life personality. There was one client who went to a lifetime as a cowboy in the Old West. This cowboy spent months at a time riding the fences, tending the cattle, with no one to talk to but his horse. Getting any kind of response from him other than a cryptic "Yup" or "Nope" was worse than pulling teeth! Another client went to a lifetime in which he had, very reluctantly, been a monk. That prior personality didn't want to be in the spiritual life and, well, it was a real ordeal to access that lifetime. The client kept saying, "I don't see anything . . . I'm just getting nothing." After I tried about every tool in my regression kit, he finally admitted: "Well, I've been seeing this monk's habit for the past fifteen minutes, and I just can't get it out of my mind!" Even in the regression, he was resistant to accepting a lifetime as a monk.

The death experience in Denise's regression is also a great example of how the initial awareness of the soul just passed over is often consistent with the religious beliefs held in the lifetime just ended. Roberto was a staunch Catholic, with great devotion to the Virgin Mary. And that was who he first saw upon death: the Virgin and Jesus. It eases the transition into the spiritual realms, where eventually all religious distinctions evaporate in the awareness of universal love. But at first, personalities often see the deities whom they worshipped during their lifetimes. Either that or they are greeted by loved ones who have preceded them in death. Some clients just go to a peaceful, loving place. It seems to depend a lot on the expectations of the personality who has just died. Whatever would be most comforting to him/her is what usually initially occurs.

Denise received some clear information about the next steps on her spiritual path from her guidance at the end of the session. It was now up to her to put this into action.

ESSENTIAL TRUTHS UNCOVERED

* Overcoming pride and feelings of superiority.
* Extending kindness and acceptance to others.

* Devoting time and attention to developing your spiritual connection.
* Opening your heart through service to others.

EXPANDING YOUR PERSPECTIVE

What is your concept of heaven or what you might experience after death? Is it based on religious beliefs or texts, or is it something more individual and personal? I asked my father this question once. To my great surprise, this rather dogmatic Midwesterner of German Catholic heritage described something more like the Native American concept of a happy hunting ground: "A place where I can walk in the woods all day with Ol' Jack [his favorite hunting dog from his youth in Wisconsin] and I don't have to work." Try exploring this question with your friends and family. They might surprise you! How do you think the different concepts of the after-death experience influence how each of us lives his/her life?

CHAPTER 23

Women's Knowledge

I HAD NOT SEEN Elaine for at least six years. She and her former husband had participated in marital therapy with me in the past. I knew their marriage had eventually ended in divorce, but I had not stayed up-to-date with Elaine. I had always appreciated her quiet energy, her spiritual approach to events in her life, and her single-minded devotion to her children. So I was somewhat taken aback when the woman who walked into my office appeared quite exhausted and dispirited, unsure of herself, and defeated by life.

The years after the divorce had been very difficult. She had essentially raised the children on her own with no financial support from their father, her ex-husband. And her children, now in their late teens, had been a real challenge to raise, posing some serious difficulties in more than one area. Elaine was looking for help in finding herself again, clarity on where to go now with her life, and assistance with how to create happiness for herself. She had lost all confidence in her ability to make wise decisions for herself and was craving guidance.

Elaine had suffered a miscarriage many years earlier, and her lack of concrete memory concerning what exactly happened then still haunted her. She chose to start her session by attempting to recover more information from that time in her current life by traveling back by hypnotic regression. When we had completed that process, and she had gained much peace of mind about that event, we proceeded to move further back to a prior lifetime. Elaine asked to see a past life where she had been her true self, where others had been good to her, and where she had made good choices.

Elaine moves very quickly into the lifetime. She finds herself dressed in white robes, and she identifies herself as a woman: "an important woman. I know how everything works," she explains with a deep, calm confidence. "I have children and a husband. They're really good people."

"Where are you?" I ask.

"I'm in Egypt; it's really beautiful here."

I prompt her to describe her role, since she has stated she is an important woman. "I'm a wife . . ." She pauses for a moment. "I lead women with women's knowledge," she continues. "The men don't want to know. But my husband knows. I know I'm important . . ." She strays a bit. "It feels good to be here. He loves me."

She focuses again and identifies herself as coming from a long line of priestesses "from aeons of time. We help a lot of people, but they don't know we help. I help on a psychic level, and I can stop the negative energy coming and turn it around . . . There are no more real spiritual teachers; everybody has to follow the rules of the priests. But the priests ignore the women's knowledge and don't want women anymore. We're still here, but they don't want to listen to us."

I'm expecting the Egyptian priestess will be angry or upset by this situation. However, when I ask her about this, she is serene and composed as she says: "No, because I know what's going to happen. I know about the great cycles, and I know where I am. I can do things. I do astrology, and I know where things are going. Currently we are in a cycle of social decay; no one wants to listen. But things will come around again."

We move forward, looking for a significant event. Her husband has died. "But I'm not sad; I know he's still here," she proclaims. "I know when I'm going to die myself."

We move to her death. All her children and grandchildren are there, and "they are amazed when they watch me die. I just glow; I just glow light. I am showing them what I taught them is real. Some of them doubt; they don't know. But I show them this is real. Here is my last lesson to them: what I said is true, we don't die—we turn into beings of light. I just get brighter and brighter until I'm gone; there's no body left."

As we process her death in that lifetime, Elaine is given a wealth of information to help in her current life. "You can't just give up, because there's no one else to teach [others]. You have to be the last teacher so we don't lose ourselves," she is advised. "I'm very strong; I can manage. I tend to forget this."

Elaine's hands start moving in the air above her, illustrating a point. "You weave it with your hands—life—all together. We'll all be together again between lives; our job is to push away bad energies and bring up good for people. That's why I'm here: learning it now so I can help others to be enlightened."

The spiritual guidance we access comforts Elaine that her children in this life are going to be fine and she'll be there for them when needed. She is encouraged not to worry about what others think, to follow her true heart. "Make decisions that are right for you; don't be led by others. Pay attention to your heart and what you tell yourself," she is told. She is advised to take time to study on her own and allow herself more alone time; to build a sacred altar and connect with her spiritual side so she does not feel alone. "They will come," the guidance assures her. "Put flowers in the room and they will come." It is clear to both of us that "they" refers to the beings of light that are waiting to work with Elaine.

A very different woman left my office from the one who entered a couple of hours earlier. It's difficult to convey in words how this session felt. The soulfulness, deep knowledge, and almost royal presence of the Egyptian priestess were truly there in the room. It was quite an honor to spend some time with her. My hope for Elaine was that she would be able to integrate the self-assurance and wisdom of the priestess into her current life.

ESSENTIAL TRUTHS UNCOVERED

* Following your heart.
* Releasing worry about what others think.
* Helping others to be enlightened.
* Knowing that your spiritual connection is a resource that is always available.

EXPANDING YOUR PERSPECTIVE

Where do you turn when you've lost your way? Often we're overwhelmed by life and its demands when we think we have to handle everything on our own. We fail to see and utilize the resources we actually have available to us. This can include something as simple as a walk in nature, writing in a journal, reading a piece of inspirational writing, talking to a counselor, meditation or spiritual practice, or maybe just a great laugh. It might be all we need to get our sense of perspective back.

Many of us are surprised to find that friends and family members are usually honored when we turn to them for help instead of us always having to be there for them. Make a list of the resources you have available to you and keep adding to it. Keep it somewhere you can refer to when life gets you down. Then avail yourself of some of your resources. None of us is meant to find our way completely on our own; by design, as they say, it takes a village.

CHAPTER 24

Advice from a Psychic Socialite

A FAIR NUMBER of people come to me because they feel they have some psychic abilities and perhaps have had some unusual experiences relating to that. They often don't know what to make of it or what, if anything, to do with their abilities. These clients are always very interesting to work with; one in particular comes to mind whose regression was absolutely fascinating. In fact, this is one of my all-time favorite stories because the past life personality that came forward was so thoroughly animated, engaging, and full of surprises.

This client came to me rather early on in my work as a regression therapist, and it was the first time that I had experienced a former personality actually talking about and giving advice to the present life personality. I conferred with a professional colleague after seeing this client, and he confirmed that when a person accesses a life of great spiritual growth, he/she can have the ability to give advice to the present personality. "It doesn't happen often, but you know you are working with a highly advanced soul, even if it is not reflected in the present lifetime," he pointed out. In other words, the client in his/her current life may not exhibit the extent of insight and understanding that the past life personality possesses.

Rita came to see me for a past life regression, mainly because she had become friends with a younger man with whom she felt a strong but at times ambivalent connection. Jeff was appearing in her dreams in many different relationship constellations: in some dreams he was her friend; in others, her father or brother; and at times he appeared as her lover. Rita worked in the high-tech field and proclaimed herself to be very "logical, left-brain oriented." However, she also admitted that strange things would happen to her. She could intuitively feel what was going on with others and would get messages about helping those who were in trouble.

Rita was very uncomfortable with these apparent psychic moments, as they fit with neither her engineer's picture of the world nor her conventional Catholic upbringing. However, some friends encouraged her to pursue a past life regression with me to see if she could make sense out of what was going on in her life. We entered our session looking for a prior lifetime in which she and Jeff had shared a significant connection. We ended up with that and more.

———

Rita's first impression is that she is standing in brown lace-up boots and wearing a loose, flowing, satin-like dress. Her hair is pulled up in many curls, and she is wearing a stylish hat with a feather. She identifies her name as Isabelle and she is twenty-nine years old. She is standing outside a "rich man's bar," watching beautiful carriages rolling by on a cobblestone street in San Francisco in 1860.

A man and woman with an infant alight from one of the carriages. The man appears to be of Spanish blood and is wearing a fine tailored black suit with a checkered neck scarf and tooled leather boots. This is Isabelle's childhood friend, Edward. His wife, Louise, is crying pitifully. "She has cheated on him, and he is turning her and her child out. He will provide for them, but he is deeply hurt and cannot stand to be around her," Isabelle explains. As a favor, Isabelle has agreed to accompany Louise to the train station to see her off.

Isabelle has loved Edward dearly since childhood. They grew up together. "I would often sneak off from lessons to meet him and play together by the water," she remembers. Despite their mutual affection, they never pursued a romantic relationship. Edward eventually married Louise, a woman Isabelle considers to be a gold digger. Isabelle herself remained single. "I developed a reserve toward men as a result of having been raped by a family friend when I was a child," she says matter-of-factly. "And my heart really belonged to Edward. I never found another who felt right." We establish that Edward is, indeed, Jeff in this lifetime.

Heartbroken after the failure of his marriage, Edward asks Isabelle to attend a dance with him. She believes that it is really too soon for him—he is still too emotionally raw—but agrees to go along nonetheless. The party is in a grand dance hall on the second story of a beautiful Victorian house decorated with glass ornaments. "I'm wearing a blue-green ball gown and have tassels in my hair. The weather is so nice, I'm not even wearing gloves!" she says, surprised. She receives many invitations to dance but turns them down, dancing only with Edward. She feels a little overwhelmed and a little tipsy. She and Edward haven't spent this much time and been this open with each other in some while.

Isabelle and Edward leave the dance floor and move off to the balcony, which looks down on the oak trees underneath and the beautiful hills in the distance. She and Edward sit on a bench with African carvings and cloth coverings. There is a full moon overhead with a ring around it. Something about the ring suddenly makes Isabelle realize that she really should not be there alone with Edward.

"Why have we grown apart?" Edward asks.

"We're only here to serve certain purposes for each other. It's not the right time for us," Isabelle replies. She feels sorry that Edward had to discover his wife's affair—with the city mayor, no less—on his own. *I knew about it; why did I not tell him?* she wonders. *Because I couldn't stop this: his heart needed to be broken,* she reflects further.

It is at this point that the nature of the regression begins to change. Isabelle starts to say more about herself. "I'm different from others," she explains. "Some say it's the devil's work; some would think that

I'm crazy like my grandmother. But this is different." Apparently her grandmother was a paranoid schizophrenic who the family viewed, understandably, as a crazy woman. "I have clairaudience: I hear spirits. I can also move objects. It's easy pushing things out of harm's way. I can help people because I very distinctly hear guidance about what they need."

Isabelle, the past life personality, starts to talk about Rita, the current life personality. "Rita has what I have but hasn't worked to develop it. Her life's path goes beyond healing [herself] and she's beginning to figure this out. She's here to help people. Her soul has attained what many strive for and has returned to help others. She's actually been doing it fairly extensively. Her family and husband see it as micromanaging, but she knows when not to interfere. She can locate things for people, too, such as when she told her friend where she left her keys. Rita hides herself too much, even from those who could understand. She needs to realize how special she is." (Rita later confirmed that a friend had lost her keys and that Rita told her exactly where to find them, even though she wasn't with her when the keys were misplaced.)

The session also enjoys a lighthearted interlude when Isabelle reflects on the San Francisco of her time versus the city today. And Berkeley—"that little tent city across the bay!"—astonishes her when she realizes what it has become. Isabelle is a delightful personality, and she bursts into giggles when she grasps that people now sometimes refer to children as "rug rats." (Remember, this regression took place quite a few years ago.)

Things take a more serious turn as Isabelle directs her attention to Rita's connection with Jeff. "The time wasn't right for me and Edward, but Jeff will be someone important for Rita," she counsels. "He can understand and help Rita as she explores her psychic abilities." Isabelle also comments on the complex dynamics in Rita's current marriage and what purposes this relationship was meant to accomplish.

Isabelle goes on to urge Rita to continue the relationship with Jeff. She herself let go of Edward before their relationship could fully develop, but Jeff is in Rita's life to ground her, to bring her comfort through the changes that are ahead of her, and to help her. She speaks of a transcendent kind of love that is the deepest of spiritual bonds, indicating this is the kind of electric connection that Rita has with Jeff. "Rita feels this but fears it," Isabelle says. "It is not the right time now, but maybe in the future. This time it is human choice."

Isabelle continues with information and advice about Rita's psychic abilities: "The whispers in her ear are messages from the guides that we [Isabelle/Rita] agreed with before birth." She indicates that Rita needs to develop a greater relationship with her spiritual guides and let go of the Catholic notions of heaven and hell. "It's all one continuous stream until we reach enlightenment. The light is not far away. Each birth we start over. The soul is in a new body, with new eyes, and learns anew." She explains that we can't know what we agreed to once we're beyond the "veil of forgetfulness," or there would be no point in learning. The real lessons come from actual experience.

"For Rita, however, it will help for her to know that she's here to help people," Isabelle asserts. "Souls grow into higher realms of enlightenment by bringing their lessons back to help others. The Dalai Lama is a good example of what we all work toward: his soul is much older than mine in terms of the wisdom he has attained."

Isabelle also gives Rita advice on many other family members as well as some friends and how to approach them. In one case she tells her to watch out for a certain fellow who is dangerous somehow, and that Rita's role will be to help stop him.

Toward the end of our session, Isabelle also addresses some comments to me. In her forthright manner, she compliments me on the path I have taken in helping people and thanks me for doing so. And then she asks me to be sure to tell Rita that she enjoyed a very happy lifetime as the daughter of a successful merchant in Rome and

Athens. I find this rather amusing, but it seems Isabelle wants to re-assure Rita that not every lifetime was filled with challenges.

Although Isabelle's life was difficult and she and Edward never played out their love for each other, she assures us that she eventually "dies old and happy." She marries later in life and has adopted children and grandchildren whom she loves.

———

About a month after the session, I heard from Rita. She had much to process from the session and was still in some turmoil over Jeff's role in her life. She confessed that she had been going through a very rough time with her husband and regretted that she had not been more revealing about him during our session. "I am afraid this is a life lesson that will not come easy," she wrote. She also confirmed that the direction Isabelle had indicated for her was not an entirely new concept; she had been battling with it for a while: "Helping others in their lives and setting people on other courses is a tough calling. Hard to accept totally, even though I suspected it in several instances."

Contact information being long out-of-date, I don't have any further follow-up to Rita's story. We can only imagine what impact Isabelle, the charming psychic socialite, had on Rita's life direction and decisions. Much of Isabelle's advice to Rita could apply to many of us.

Isabelle had some important observations on life and rebirth: how liberating it is to see each new lifetime as a fresh beginning for the soul to learn anew; to drop old concepts of heaven and hell and realize that we are on a continuous stream of learning until we reach enlightenment. This is why we often forget the plans we made for ourselves from the spiritual plane before this lifetime so we can learn anew from direct experience, the most effective teacher.

This story also points out some important considerations about relationships. At times, our purpose with a loved one is limited, and, once accomplished, we are meant to move on. Isabelle realized that she could not stop Edward from learning about his wife's affair and having his heart broken, because that would have interfered with his development. It is so difficult not to want to jump in and shield those we love from a painful experience, yet doing so could rob them of their own learning and growth.

As Isabelle asked me to assure Rita, it is helpful to know that not every lifetime has been filled with difficulty and angst; generally those are the lifetimes that come up in a regression, because we usually are asking for the source of a problem or issue. And even as Isabelle experienced, a challenging early life can still lead to happiness and fulfillment later on.

ESSENTIAL TRUTHS UNCOVERED

* Releasing old definitions of heaven and hell, and realizing that we are on an ongoing journey toward enlightenment.
* Accepting that not all relationships are meant to be permanent; their purpose may be limited in this lifetime, although extensive in another.
* Gaining patience in learning from experience; seeing each event in life as an opportunity to grow as a person.
* Building eventual happiness despite difficulties early in life.

EXPANDING YOUR PERSPECTIVE

The daily struggles that life presents are opportunities to cultivate spiritual growth. Not just living our experience but learning from it is a key message in this chapter. This takes patience, acceptance, and a willingness to trust that everything will work out to the greater good, despite appearances at the time. Often with the 20/20 vision of hindsight, we are able to see the good that grew out of a difficult situation over which we were despairing when it originally occurred.

To strengthen this realization, contemplate those especially difficult times you have faced in your life. What did you think about each one then, and what do you think about it now with that 20/20 hindsight? What benefit or learning evolved out of that struggle? If you jot these thoughts down in your journal, you can remind yourself of this perspective when facing challenges in the future.

CHAPTER 25

What's the Point?

MAYBE BECAUSE WE often forget the plans we make on the spiritual plane prior to this life, the question "What is my life purpose?" comes up for people at many ages and stages of their lives. Some will seek past life regression work to get a better handle on this. Often, like Jill, these clients are in midlife. Having enjoyed career success, they are looking for more fulfillment with a potential new direction in their lives. At times I have clients in their twenties, just starting out their adult lives, who want to make sure they are following the right path. And I have even worked with people in their sixties and seventies who, approaching the latter stages of their lives, feel something is missing and are still wondering just what their purpose is in this lifetime. I firmly believe it's never too late to make an adjustment and pursue something with heart, meaning, and passion.

The focus of Jill's life, until recently, was her career. She had a very responsible management position and described her life as having been easy until about five years earlier, when she married for the first time. Unexpected difficulties arose with her new husband, and Jill also suffered a miscarriage, which was shattering for her. She and her husband were working on their marriage, but Jill was still struggling to understand what she had been through in a larger context. She was looking for deeper meaning and purpose in her life.

The question she posed for her regression was "What's the point of this lifetime?"

It takes a moment for Jill to settle into her regression. Her initial impressions are of flashes with "everything covered in white, like it's bright and new." I instruct her to imagine a wonderful hallway opening before her with one particular door that beckons to her. Jill describes this door as medieval in appearance, with wood planks and a heavy metal handle. (With this technique, the design of the door is often a clue to the lifetime we are about to enter.) As I have her go through the door, she finds herself on a dark stone stairway spiraling downward. This stairway takes her to a courtyard on street level.

The dirt courtyard is surrounded by large, well-built stone buildings with windows and pointed towers. Most of the buildings are homes, and there are also a few shops. "There's a donkey . . . someone's with the donkey . . . It may be me!" she exclaims.

As I have Jill connect with the person in that scene, she identifies as a man about thirty years old, wearing a simple white tunic. He is walking with the donkey and at first he says he is barefoot, but then says, "there's some leather under my soles, like sandals." He feels healthy, tall, wiry, and physically strong. "I'm comfortable here," he says. "I have nice things. I like my body. I like myself."

I inquire about the location and date: Romania about the year 1725 is his answer.

The young man mentions that an older man, someone important, is coming to mind. The older man is short, stout, and wears a vest. Our main character describes him as "compact and funny," and when I ask about the relationship between the two of them, he thinks they're family somehow.

As is sometimes true in regressions, information comes through in more than one way. "I hear 'leather,'" he says, and repeats that he has "nice things." Gradual understanding develops about the role of this older man. "He's my father—but I'm more successful than him.

He's so warm. It's a good relationship." He sees his father's mustache, bushy eyebrows, and bright blue eyes, and we identify this individual as the same being as Jill's father in her current life.

"He's made very nice leather things for me; he's an artist," the son proclaims proudly. As for himself, he does something with land: he's an administrator or buyer for estates. "I own some land myself," he says, "but I'm not that old," implying that he has time to build his holdings.

I instruct him to jump to a significant event in that lifetime. Immediately he reports being in a dark place, like a dungeon or basement, and there's moss growing on stone walls. He isn't restrained, but he's sad. "I shouldn't be here," he laments. "I'm around forty and stuck here. I see myself putting my hands on the wall and feeling so very sad." Interestingly, he also comments that he's more "yellow" and mentions that he can only see a little sun through the grate over a small, square window. It appears he's been away from the sunlight for a while.

When I probe for the reason that he is imprisoned, the information comes out piecemeal and the images are described as being almost "cartoon-like." There's a dinner party. Next thing he knows, he's falling on the ground; something about his legs and being attacked by an angry dark-haired man. "Things are easy for me, people like me," he explains. But this other man, "he has to take things; he doesn't know how to earn. He takes by force."

"I have curly brown hair . . . Women like me," he continues with an apparent non sequitur. Wondering if this fight is about a woman, I ask if there's a particular lady in his life. He describes a woman with red-blond hair, frizzy and long. Her eyes are hazel and her skin is ruddy and freckled. "She's very simple, not smart," he says, not unkindly, "but she's so warm and she knows things about plants. We're together; she's my wife. We're happy."

He now understands that this dinner party is their wedding feast. The other man is looking at his wife with jealousy. This man wants her for himself. "He's so dark, his energy and his looks!" he says, and then comes the realization that this is his brother. He's darker and shorter than our main character, and there's "something wrong, with either his body or his mind," he observes. We identify the brother as Jill's husband in her current life.

The brother is angry over many things. "I ignored him a lot," he admits. "He deserved something that I took or didn't care about. I could have shared, taken more time, taken him places. He's younger, but especially in his head," he observes, implying a mental or emotional immaturity.

We return to the incident in which his brother attacks him. He can't seem to move his legs, and a knife is involved. "We hurt each other; we always do!" he declares. "We fought frequently, but our arms are together; we're always linked."

After the injury "I go away alone. I don't feel close to my wife anymore. I just want to be alone. I'm scared and different somehow from what happened," he explains. "I'm changed. I'm not arrogant anymore. I was young, careless, entitled.

"What my brother did may have been right—I deserved it. I love him still. I took something from him—not the girl, I took something so he couldn't be who he was supposed to be. I owe him something."

This seems unclear, so I probe further to identify exactly what was taken. He is finally able to pinpoint the issue: "I took love. I made him feel bad. My brother needed me and I didn't care."

When we jump to the next significant event, he is living alone in a little house very peacefully. He has enough money and is able to read, write, and learn. "I go outside my body a lot; I meditate a lot," he says. "I'm older now; I feel OK—lucky, even. I gave my brother much of what I had after the fight. I woke up and didn't want it anymore. I was drunk, went to jail for a bit, then made amends. He needed and wanted money and stuff more than me. I wanted to go higher—[but] not [in] the material world . . . I study, read, and learn spiritually. I'm a monk, but not church related. I know things."

Moving forward, our self-proclaimed monk is alone for a long time. Then a girl shows up who wants to learn from him; he identifies her as his spiritual daughter. "I'm going to die soon so I need to give the knowledge to someone else. I have a lot of knowledge, more than the local people. It's a knowing inside you, not someone telling you how to understand. Sit quietly and learn differently on different levels. Go higher and higher."

On his final day he knows he's about to die. He's in his little house and a lady who occasionally cares for him is there. "I'm so happy! I feel energy, a force going up. I know how it will feel," he says. He's about seventy, which is considered a very long life and uncommon at that time. People from the village are outside. "They think I'm a saint, but I'm not!" he asserts. "I would talk to them, put my hands on them, and tell them simple things away from what is destructive against the self. Most people only hurt themselves. I show them there is no evil in the world outside them, even though they think there is." At the moment of death, he rises up and into the light and feelings of love. "I feel I had a good life," he concludes.

Processing this life experience and accessing wisdom from the higher realms is very rich for Jill. Some interesting lessons emerge: first, about releasing selfishness, the judgment of others, and being too self-centered. "Even in learning I was alone too much; I didn't share enough—not just materially but giving of the self." She identifies the past personality as being too hyperfocused rather than integrated, and that he could have stepped up to do more difficult things, since learning was so easy for him.

Jill recognizes a similar hyperfocus in her current life, in which she goes intensely into one thing, then drops it for the next interest. She also sees herself as being alone too much and at times feeling a bit separate from others. "Not many people are like me," she observes. She sees her challenge as learning to be happy in the present and to integrate it all now, although she does express some worry at the ramifications of "going higher" and if that would separate her too much from human life.

A spirit guide appears to Jill in the form of a combined man/hawk figure. The guide tells her that she can have "another life" in her current lifetime—that she will live a long time and she can connect more to people and to knowledge. But "no more games; you play too many games," he admonishes. "You don't have to pretend anymore like you don't know [what you know]."

Regarding her marriage, the existence of a loving connection between her and her husband (her brother in the former life) is reaffirmed, with the need for patience and understanding that each has a timetable in his/her own evolution.

Addressing Jill's continued grief over her miscarriage and the feeling that she deserves to be a mother, the man/hawk guide tells her, "It's life: you can't control it. The child has free will too. The meaning isn't in having the child; it's in making life beautiful even without her. There is no 'deserve.'"

Jill's realizations in this between-lives space become more esoteric: "I can access these things all the time. There's a big tower of knowledge—all levels, all places—all around me. I can pull strings of knowledge from me to others at work and link them to the tower. I hide it, but I don't need to hide knowledge . . . I only need to give people a little piece of knowledge and then they can get it by themselves."

At the end of her time in the spiritual realms, Jill is told by her guide to "go up and see how everything works and wraps around everything else."

I think this story is a wonderful illustration of the regression process and how it often feels a little like an intriguing detective story. Information had to be teased out slowly, and it took a while for the whole story about the conflict with the brother to emerge. This is one of the things that make my work so interesting for me. I never quite know where a session is going to go. Just like life, surprising things come up when you least expect them.

The change of life direction that Jill experienced in the former lifetime was quite dramatic. Her current life showed some reflections of that change in focus—from achievement and material success to relationship and spirituality—but in a more moderate and integrated way. The man/hawk guide that appeared to her was quite pointed in encouraging her to open up even more, delve into that higher knowledge that she could access easily, and share that knowledge with others. This is something that had only been done when approaching death in the prior life, but it appeared to be an important component of her mission now.

Jill also received some comfort and reassurance about her marriage and her pain over the miscarriage. The ties between her and her husband were strong ("We're always linked") despite the conflict between them. It boded well for their future together, and resolving that pattern of conflict now might mean that the need for conflict in future lives together will be eliminated.

Losing a child through miscarriage is devastating: I speak from personal experience on this. The guide's comments about the child's free will and there being no "deserve" puts the experience in a different context. Difficult as it is to lose those we love, it often isn't really about us and our needs and wants. We must grieve, find acceptance, and then determine to move forward and make life beautiful. That is a way to honor the loss.

Often clients inquiring about life purpose want specific advice on a career path or how to contribute professionally to the world. At times they get what they ask for, as we saw with our Renaissance man in Chapter 4. He was advised to return to Asia and to see law as just a stepping-stone to other humanistic pursuits. Other times, as we see here, a client is guided more toward a way of being in the world. Typically the lessons that come through focus on the need to love ourselves, the need to love and help each other, the need to let go and trust the process.

Especially when I work with a younger client on life purpose, there is such human impatience in the process. So many times we just want the answer to what our specific talents and gifts are and how we are supposed to use them in the world. But these talents and gifts are often developed in the process of searching, in the dilemma of not knowing. If we try to know our end point before we've walked the path, we might very possibly miss the point of the journey and end up in an entirely different place. And as I've heard more than once in session, the point isn't what you do; the point is to mean something to the souls around you while you do it. It appears that Jill had the capacity to greatly expand the positive influence she could have on the lives of those around her, and that was a potential she was being encouraged to embrace more fully in her current life.

ESSENTIAL TRUTHS UNCOVERED

* Letting go of self-destructive habits and attitudes.
* Sharing both materially and of yourself.
* Creating meaning by making life beautiful despite losses.
* Accessing higher knowledge to help yourself and others.
* Impacting the people around you in positive ways.

EXPANDING YOUR PERSPECTIVE

I have a quote above the little altar area I use for meditation, from the well-known thirteenth-century Persian poet and Sufi mystic Rumi: "Wherever you stand, be the soul of that place." What would life be like if this were the guiding principle each of us followed? In what simple ways can you expand the positive influence you have on those around you in your daily life by bringing your soulful awareness to your surroundings?

CHAPTER 26

Cherishing Life

LORRAINE WAS AN energetic woman in her mid-fifties who had been a teacher for many years. She had faced many challenges within her own family, particularly with a son who was battling alcoholism. This had drained Lorraine's emotional resources, and in fact she was now facing her own serious health challenge. However, she was maintaining some kind of balance through all of these issues by meditating regularly and following a spiritual program. When she came to see me for a past life session, rather than focusing on the problems with her son or her health, she wanted to keep it wide-open and see whatever was most significant for her at that time. Lorraine proved to be very adept at accessing good detail within the prior lifetime and maneuvering easily in the interlife space.

Lorraine's first impressions are of bare feet on warm sand and a soft white fabric that moves fluidly at her knees with lower legs bare. A blue fabric on top hangs over the shoulders. As we move our attention upward, a male face comes into focus. With slightly rough features in a roundish face, he has bright, startling green eyes surrounded by dark eyelashes and eyebrows, a short beard, and long dark brown hair that is pulled back. His skin is a brownish color. I ask him how old he is, and he says about thirty. He describes himself as "outdoorsy, muscular from working and building."

I ask what he builds, and he says he builds walls from stone. His hands are rough from the work. "It feels good to build, to work, to accomplish," he states. I ask what name he goes by, and he says he is called Jennis. However, he cannot identify his location other than "in a valley," and as far as the year, he has no idea, because "no one cares."

Jennis tells me that he builds for the other people in his small community: "families that we care about." He also builds for protection, from both animals and other people who might threaten them. The area is very open, and there is a river around them that runs very deep. "Others use the river for travel, but we use the shallow water only," he says. "We don't swim in it. We must take care of the children, because they can get lost in the water."

I ask Jennis to take me to the structure where he lives. It's a stone house with a stone floor, and with fabric for the door and window coverings. The roof is wood. "I didn't build the house," he tells me. His "woman," Myla, is there. "She's very pretty, but no green eyes," he says. "Myla's are brown." They have been together many years, since they were very young. Most of the time they are happy with each other, he explains pragmatically, and he describes her as strong and happy. When I check to see if Myla is someone that Lorraine knows in her current life, she is identified as Lorraine's current grandson.

There is an old lady who also lives with them: Jennis's maternal grandmother. She helps with the house, cooks, and is rather cranky, according to Jennis. "She had many children," he explains. "She likes me, says I'm handsome and fun. I think she wants to be taken care of; living isn't easy." The grandmother is identified as a good friend of Lorraine's in her current life.

Jennis and Myla have a number of young children. The younger girl is about four years old, and the older girl is ten. Jennis tells me that there was another girl in between those two, but she died. He also has two sons who are somewhat older. The elder son is in his teens and lives close by with his woman. The younger son no longer lives at home, either, but is working for Jennis's brother in the same village.

There is quite a bit of family around, and Jennis really appreciates this fact. He married into this community and doesn't travel much from its surroundings. His brother's woman is from a place with trees, he notes. "It's a long walk there." And his older daughter is overly obsessed, in his mind, with what else there is in the world: "She's too adventurous for a girl; we need her help! She is independent, strong willed, and stubborn." She is identified as a fellow teacher and very close friend in Lorraine's current life.

I have Jennis return to the original scene, in which he is standing barefoot in the warm sand. He observes that the sun is changing, moving toward the summer. The grass is very green, the plants are growing, and the river is high. This means more food because of the multitude of fish in the river. He points out that "we need to be careful about the animals. The big ones hunt our small animals; some of the smaller ones give milk." He adds that when it's green, as it is now, there will be lots of milk from these small animals.

As we move forward, Jennis comes to a scene where he sees flowers all around. They are outside celebrating the birth of his brother's daughter's baby, his great-niece. "It is very important when a baby is born to welcome it, share food, and sing," he says. "Some babies don't live; we don't understand why." Everyone in the community is included in the celebration. There are thirty to forty people, including children and elders. "The people are kind to the old ones," he remarks.

Jennis gives me more of his personal history. He has been building walls since he was very young. His son now does the rock shaping, and Jennis acknowledges that he is very good at it. "My son is also very funny. He makes things, teases the children, is tricky," he says. This son is identified as one of Lorraine's former students in her current life, a student she was very fond of.

Jennis mentions that "they always marveled at my eyes. I came from somewhere else when I was very young; the old ones know." It appears he was with his mother and a number of other people traveling in a small boat when it capsized and everyone except him and his mother drowned. The people he is now living with pulled the two of them out of the water: "I could walk, but I was very small," he recalls.

Jennis continues to relate his tale: "My mother also had green eyes, and there were two men interested in her." She was frightened, however, not knowing these people who spoke a different language, and an older lady, whom Jennis now calls his grandmother, took her in. The men slept outdoors, courting her. Jennis's mother decided she didn't care much for one of the men, so the old lady ran him off. His mother eventually joined with the other man and had more children by him. When Jennis was older, he gained his own sleeping place. Myla, his friend from childhood, joined him as his woman.

I ask Jennis to move to the next significant event after the birth of his great-niece. We skip over a long stretch of time: "I'm an old man; my eyes don't see, and Myla's gone! It was old age, but it was a shock." Jennis now lives with a grandson, in a small stone house attached to his grandson's house.

"People come and go more now," Jennis says. "More people travel on the river now; even my grandson does it." I ask how he spends his time now that he is old and blind: "I walk along my walls," he replies. "I can find my way around. I tell stories, open nuts [for the children]. But my hands are tired and sore. I wonder what will happen to the people around here—will they stay?" He believes that his grandson, who wants to get away and explore the world, will probably leave when he dies. "Now I wonder what I missed about travel and about the world," he muses.

We go to Jennis's last day of life. He is outside, feeling the sun. The sounds are fading. "I keep asking to 'go home'; I'm ready to die. I know everyone will be okay," he says reassuringly. "There's something special, somewhere I belong." His death is peaceful and quiet.

"It's beautiful; there are so many beings with me. They are wrapping me in light." As we process the lifetime of Jennis the stoneworker, we identify a number of worthwhile lessons. He learned to lose the fear of unknown people and to feel worthy in himself. Caring for others was key: both feeling that concern and acting upon it. A significant realization was to understand that many things—including other people—were out of his control. And finally, a key lesson was to never fear death.

I ask Lorraine how the life of Jennis is pertinent to her current life. Why did this lifetime come up as the most important one for her to see today? She is able to identify a number of relevant correlations between Jennis's experiences and her own in the present life. The first is to be comfortable with who you are, even if you look or sound different from others. The acceptance of loss is also a big theme in both lives, with the recognition that things aren't necessarily taken from you; things just change. There is also the realization from both life experiences that all the worrying and feeling responsible for outcomes is unnecessary. "You have no control; life can be simple if you let it," she asserts. Finally, Lorraine notes that both lives demonstrate that you do not have to be so serious or take things too personally in order to do a good job with your life.

We have already received a lot of good information, but there is more to come as I direct Lorraine to focus on the presence of a very wise and loving being who is there to counsel and advise her: her spiritual guide. This is what she is told: "Cherish the human life; care for and encourage it. Remember, you've done it before. Work on patience, especially with yourself. Remember you are loved. Know that the love is always there. It pours in; it is strong.

"You have had many lifetimes with Myla (Jennis's wife/Lorraine's grandson). There is a strong bond around the enjoyment of spirituality, creating strong bonds, helping each other. Myla is actually one of your guiding ones. You may not always be on the planet together, but you will be working together anyway.

"Rejoice in your current life. Remember a simpler time, make it easier, gather the joy, and hang on. It is your choice whether to go or stay [in this life, referring to her health challenges], and it is okay to not choose for now. Some things have to wait for the moment."

———

Lorraine apparently chose to stay. She returned for another regression six and a half years later. The situation with her son had eventually resolved wonderfully, and he was married and in recovery. Her own health situation was also successfully resolved. She had another lovely regression that also resulted in some very deeply felt spiritual communication at the end:

"Total complete divine love is there. You can use your free will and use it [the divine love] for strength and goodness wherever it is needed. Know that you have that, and your beloved ones. It's completely wonderful."

And so it is. If we are able to open to the divine reality of our existence, our enduring connections with our loved ones across many lifetimes, and the depth of divine love pouring into us every moment of our lives, it is completely wonderful. We just need to remember.

ESSENTIAL TRUTHS UNCOVERED

* Feeling your own worth without fearing others.
* Extending caring to others while understanding that you can't control them.
* Accepting loss with the understanding that things just change, they aren't taken from you.
* Releasing the fear of death.
* Realizing that you can do well in life even as you take things less seriously and less personally.

EXPANDING YOUR PERSPECTIVE

A former teacher of mine in the yogic tradition expressed the continuous cycle of consciousness as follows: "We are It; we forget we are It; we remember; we are It." What things cause you to forget your divine nature: Bad commute traffic? Sick kids? Money troubles? Keep an eye out for these triggers and see if you can catch yourself from falling into forgetfulness as quickly as you might have in the past.

What things help you to remember your connection to the divine or something bigger than yourself? Many people find that regular meditation or a centering practice is essential to keeping their emotional and spiritual balance. It doesn't have to be a long period of time as classic schools of meditation require. Make it something easy, enjoyable, and most of all doable for you. Even if it's five minutes sitting and following your breath, listing what you are grateful for, or petting your dog as you think about his/her loving nature—any of these practices can help you stay in remembering mode when you do them on a regular basis. I invite you to try a regular centering practice if you don't already have one.

CONCLUSION:

CLOSING THE FILES

I HAVE TREASURED my work with past life clients over the years. I have been captivated and often profoundly moved by the personal stories of these prior lifetimes. As my files of case studies continued to expand, it just kept hitting me that not only were these stories fascinating, there was an amazing amount of spiritual knowledge embedded within each of them; they had to be shared with a larger audience. Also, as an avid reader of historical fiction, these case studies have intrinsic value to me: it's intriguing to learn about what people wore, what they ate, how they lived, and what their particular worldviews were, in their own words.

Although a belief in reincarnation is not necessary to enjoy and benefit from these case studies, it certainly enhances a deeper appreciation of them and how they reflect the dynamics in the clients' current lives. Understanding that we are eternal beings, manifesting on the physical plane over and over again in different human bodies and personalities, brings such enrichment to our current lifetimes. It expands our vision of life and what it means to be human. It enhances our understanding of what our purpose is here on the planet. It certainly has eliminated the fear of death for many, many clients. It assuages our feeling of loss when we see how we have been with loved ones before and will be with them again. And it richly magnifies our relationships with the people in our lives, particularly when we see the chains of love and connection that have endured across lifetimes.

Moving client after client through prior lifetimes and what comes between lifetimes offers a unique perspective on death and the connections between ourselves and those we love. Once death is met, a client's ongoing awareness moves into the realization that we continue without the physical body, we are connected to those we love at all times, and we are connected to all of existence. The loss of a loved one in any lifetime is no longer seen as a permanent loss but rather as a temporary suspension of shared experience on the physical plane. It can, of course, be extremely painful at the time. But with our own deaths, the trials and tribulations, the grief, the loss from any particular lifetime, drop away as a temporary human drama as our consciousness expands back to the eternal realities that uphold all of life. In the words of Natalie, whom you may remember from Chapter 11: "Life takes on a whole new meaning when you look at it as your soul's journey."

Sometimes we forget how limited our physical perceptions are as human beings. Yet there is so much more than what meets our five senses. Take our vision, for example. We see colors because our eyes have three color receptors: red, green, and blue. And then there is a marine creature called the mantis shrimp that has sixteen photoreceptors in its eyes. This incredibly complex visual system enables it to see ultraviolet, visible, and polarized light. We can't even imagine the colors the mantis shrimp sees: they're beyond our human perception entirely. Yet these colors must exist or the mantis shrimp would not have evolved such an elaborate eye structure. What other realities are out there beyond our human perceptions? What can we do to aid ourselves in expanding our vision?

As I've mentioned throughout *The Past Life Perspective*, there are many ways that we can magnify our own awareness of the influence of prior lifetimes in normal daily life. If you've worked through the

"Expanding Your Perspective" sections, you've already seen many of them. We can look for clues in a number of areas: people who play a significant role in your life today; new people you meet to whom there is an immediate positive or negative reaction; areas of the world, cultures, foods, and foreign languages toward which you have an affinity; time periods that fascinate you; skills that come naturally. It's rare for these things to come straight out of the blue. Both strongly positive and strongly negative reactions can often be linked to a prior life experience.

As I pointed out in "Expanding Your Perspective" in Chapter 2, it is also common for past life material to emerge in our dreams. Pay particular attention to recurring dreams that involve a specific situation, scene, or person. This could be an experience from a prior lifetime trying to emerge, as was the case for Jonah. Traveling to different parts of the world is also an excellent way to stir up past life memories. One client reported that, upon visiting Paris for the first time, she instinctively knew exactly where everything was and how to get there—no guidebook needed. This certainly suggests a prior lifetime in which she was intimately familiar with Paris. For myself, my links to ancient Egypt were confirmed when touring in Egypt a few years ago. When visiting the Karnak temple complex in Thebes, the Temple of Isis at Philae, and the shores of the Mediterranean in Alexandria, I felt as if I was coming home on some profound level. I was also gifted with some spontaneous past life recall and a number of intense experiences of spiritual connection while there.

Of course, for those who are interested in delving deeper into their prior lifetimes, I have provided a recommended resources section in the appendices. A good option is to seek the services of a professional regression therapist, and in fact this is the approach I would recommend rather than trying do-it-yourself regressions. As you have seen from the preceding stories, there often are some dramatic and upsetting events that come up in regression. It's best to have a qualified counselor as your guide on these journeys into the past who can help you move through the traumatic events, process them, find closure, and integrate the lessons into your current life. It's not optimal to open up these kinds of memories and leave them hanging.

Most past life explorers wonder if they will be successful at retrieving a prior lifetime when they have their first regression. This is another reason it's important to work with a qualified guide. Over the years, I've learned that there is no one approach that will work well for every client. It's important to read the situation and modify the approach, depending on the individual in front of me. If progressive relaxation doesn't work for one person, it's time to reach into the tool kit and try something else. Persistence usually pays off.

It's also hard to know in advance how well someone is going to be able to do the work. I have had clients come in who have meditated daily for years, have done quite a bit of personal counseling work, and yet are completely blocked in doing a regression. One client who described herself as a very fertile dreamer did not retrieve any information in session, but that night had a past life dream that spoke directly to her inquiry. (I had suggested to her that she tell her unconscious mind upon going to bed that she would like to dream about the prior life in question. She called me the next morning very excited. Not only had it worked, but she'd gotten quite a bit of detail.) I have also had young people come in who have seemingly done very little work on themselves, have little insight into their situation, and dive right away into a profound regression experience. Always keeps me guessing!

Over the years, having kept a detailed database, I have found that an average of only 14 percent of my clients did not retrieve a past life memory. These clients fall into two main categories. First, a certain number of people want to give a regression a try despite the fact that they have a very hard time relaxing in their normal life. They are too anxious, too ramped up, too distracted by daily concerns, to let go for even a short while and relax. Typically the session, which can still be very useful, rightfully ends up focusing on their current life anxieties and difficulties—more of a conventional counseling session. The second category is made up of people for whom going into a past life would actually not be of service. The issue they bring in really is about current life situations and dynamics, or it's not the right time yet for them to retrieve the memory. In this case, we typically regress to a childhood memory from the current life or some imagery related to the issue they have brought in. I always trust that clients will go where they need to go, and if it won't be in their best interest to investigate a prior lifetime, then their unconscious mind will know that.

If we look at these statistics from the opposite viewpoint, it means that close to 90 percent of my clients have retrieved past life memories. Typically, people who have had a regular meditation or relaxation practice move most quickly into a past life regression experience. This shows that it is a skill that can be learned. The more you practice, the more detailed your experiences will be and the more easily memories will be recovered. However, there are also people who have never done any meditation, yoga, qigong, or the like who recover detailed information quickly and easily. The only way to know how it works for you is to give it a try with an open mind. So if you are interested in doing a regression, I encourage you to find a qualified past life therapist and pursue it!

I recall the story of a wise old man who, when questioned on his unfailing religious beliefs in the face of no concrete truth, responded: "If my faith causes me to live a better life, be a better person, live with more meaning, then it doesn't matter if it's true. It has fulfilled its purpose." That, in the end, is what I consider to be the great litmus test for our beliefs. If we live a richer, fuller, more love-filled life as a result of our beliefs, then hang on to them and don't worry about whether they're scientifically provable. In the final analysis, no matter how many lifetimes we have had—nine, ninety-nine, or just one—what we now have to work with is our current lives, our current bodies, and our current personalities. It is a unique, onetime experience to be this particular individual, giving expression to the life force with one's own distinctive talents and limitations, likes and dislikes, personality and characteristics. Because even though the soul essence animating this personality goes on forever, the particular individual that each of us is now will not be repeated. So find the beliefs that make this the biggest, most engaging life your unique personality can enjoy. Explore the full potential of your current personality; that's why you are here. For many people that includes an awareness and integration of their prior personalities that have contributed to the present ones, and the continuing saga of the life lessons and love connections that are being expressed.

I want to close with a profound thank-you to all the amazing people who have come to see me over the years to explore their prior lifetimes. They have exhibited a remarkable amount of courage and depth of character in doing this work. I appreciate all their willingness to have their stories shared with the world at large. It has truly been an honor to be able to live my purpose by helping others to get a glimpse beyond the physical, to expand their perspective to include the deeper realities of their existence.

A Closing Parable: How Many Lifetimes Will It Take?

There was a woman walking down a trail that many meditators were known to frequent. She noticed a meditator sitting near the path, and she heard him speaking to the sky: "How many more lifetimes do I need to meditate before I realize you, God?" he asked. The woman was shocked to hear a voice speaking out of the ether, saying, "See that bush over there? For as many leaves as are on that bush, that's how many lifetimes you will need to meditate until you realize Me!"

The meditator looked at the bush and said, "What? There are three leaves on that bush! It's going to take me *three more lifetimes*?

But I've been meditating for *so many* lifetimes already!" And the discouraged man mournfully returned to his meditation practice.

The woman was a beginning meditator herself, having practiced only a few months. She gathered up the courage to ask the same question: "How many lifetimes will it take for *me* to realize your True Nature?" The resounding voice spoke to her, "See that tree over there? For as many leaves that are on that tree, that's how many lifetimes it will take you to realize my True Nature."

The woman looked over and saw that the tree was filled with hundreds if not thousands of leaves. She cried out with great joy, "Only that many lifetimes! Oh, thank you, God; you are so compassionate to me! I love you so much; I want only You!" She began to dance around the tree, round and round, exclaiming, "Thank you, God! I love you, God!" For a long time she continued her dance around the tree in joyful ecstasy.

The leaves began to slowly fall off the tree until there was not a single leaf left.

———

With thanks to Bill Wilson, minister of Gavilan Hills Unity Church, in Gilroy, California, for sharing this parable, its origin being somewhat lost. I invite you all to enjoy the journey to enlightenment and realizing your true nature as an eternal being expressing in human form, in whatever way it comes for you!

ACKNOWLEDGMENTS

FIRST AND FOREMOST I want to thank my enlightened publisher, Zhena Muzyka, of Enliven Books. She believed enough in the mission and message in *The Past Life Perspective* to take a chance on a first-time, unproven author. Similarly, this project never would have gotten past the self-publishing stage without the vision and contribution of my wonderful agent, Lenore Skomal, of Whimsy Literary Agency, LLC, as well as the savvy and guidance of Whimsy's principal, Jackie Meyer. You are a dynamic trio of women to have in my camp as I bring my work to a larger stage.

Many thanks to Robert Stuberg of Success.bz for the coaching he provided, which was instrumental in getting me to actually sit down and write instead of just giving it lip service. Without your enthusiastic encouragement for my project and your imposition of deadlines, I don't know how many more years would have passed before I produced an actual manuscript. Joann Rompella, freelance copy editor, did a wonderful job on the initial manuscript; you gave me a laugh when you told me you were sure I had been educated in Catholic schools (I wasn't) because you usually didn't see that quality of writing on the first pass. Your improvements to that writing were sincerely appreciated!

Similarly, Emily Han, my developmental editor, turned a good manuscript into something well polished and deserving of the larger venue of an international publishing house. Thank you, Emily: you made *The Past Life Perspective* an even better book under a very tight schedule.

Angela Stoner of Bearly Marketing has been a gem, dragging me out of the Dark Ages as far as social media marketing goes. You always handled my questions with patience and good humor. Nicki Thomas of Veteran PR was very helpful with initial publicity and getting my name out to the media even before we had a book to promote. Emi Battaglia (Emi Battaglia Public Relations, LLC), with her expertise in the publishing world and extensive media contacts, was just the right fit to launch *The Past Life Perspective* into the public arena. Yona Deshommes and Arielle Kane, in-house publicity and marketing experts for Atria Books, were equally invaluable. Thank you to all my "promo" ladies, as well as the many people at Simon & Schuster who so enthusiastically embraced my work and this book.

On the more personal side, I have a number of very precious friends and family members who have given me support, encouragement, and an emotional base over the years. First, my amazing daughter, Emily Barham, with whom I am so thrilled to be sharing another lifetime. You pushed me to redefine myself at age forty when I became a mother for the first time, and again when you left home to start your college career. Your resounding "You can do it, Mom!" when I feel pushed a little too far outside my comfort zone always heartens me. I love you beyond measure.

Boundless thanks also to my husband, Dr. Robert Barham, world-class broccoli and watermelon breeder and entrepreneur. You embody outside-the-box thinking, and you continually encourage me to think bigger than I would on my own. I know sometimes I grumble, "No more ideas!," but your input in invaluable. Keep an eye out for those tornados, my dear!

My soul sisters, Eileen Lindsay-Boll and Sue Adams: there is love and understanding between us that go way beyond words. Thank you for being in my life! My "baby" sister, Dr. Susan Conrad, linguistics professor and author of many textbooks: someday, maybe, we'll write that murder mystery together! My dear friend Randi Larsen, my very first manuscript reader: as an amazing writer yourself, your seal of approval meant so much. My friend and clairvoyant Shelia Thomas, who has kept me connected with "the other side," and Tess Pierson, EFT coach, who helped me blast away some very old limiting beliefs: you are both important parts of my support system. Buddies Nancy Miller and Tess Rogers, who particularly cheered me on throughout the search for an agent and publisher; your belief was so helpful!

My entire Scolastico family played such an essential part in my development—there are too many of you to name you all individually—with special thanks to Susan Scolastico for carrying on Ron's work and providing the glue for us all. And big hugs in particular to Margie Bennett, Eileen Johnson, Leslie Hill, Mary Reed, and Jenette Rasker for your encouragement when reading my very first client stories and/or showing up to support me in my first larger venue workshop. I love you all.

Heartfelt gratitude goes to Abdallah Mohammed Abdallah of Luxor, Egypt, mystic and tour guide extraordinaire, who recognized me and kept sending me the message that I needed to share my light with the world. Our meeting in Egypt was far from chance and my experiences there were transformative. Thank you for keeping me in your heart across the miles and the years.

And I can't forget my gang of tennis buddies who help me stay sane and in the now by whacking that little fuzzy yellow ball. In fact, I'd like to acknowledge the game of tennis itself. After all, in what other situation, when you have no points at all, do they actually say you have "love"? What a reminder.

Lastly, boundless thanks to those people without whom this book never would have existed: my amazing clients! You have shown a tremendous amount of courage and fortitude to dig deep into the unknown realms of your consciousness. Thank you for trusting me with your process. And thank you for being willing to share your stories with the world at large. Yours is an important contribution to a broader awakening.

APPENDIX A:

SUGGESTED RESOURCES FOR

FURTHER EXPLORATION

AFTER READING *The Past Life Perspective*, you may be wondering what other resources are available if you want to explore further. Here are my recommendations:

For your own individualized past life session with a qualified therapist, check with the International Board for Regression Therapy (IBRT). The board maintains a directory of practitioners who have met rigorous criteria to be certified as a regression therapist. I strongly suggest that you select someone who has counseling in addition to hypnosis credentials, so if traumatic material comes up, you are guided by someone who is trained in these matters. A number of us now offer sessions over Skype, so distance need not be a barrier. **www.IBRT.org**

The *International Journal of Regression Therapy*, formerly a practitioners-only publication, has been made accessible to everyone via the Internet through the efforts of the Earth Association for Regression Therapy. You can access free abstracts and introductions from professional articles written by prominent past life practitioners. If one of the articles interests you, you can then buy it online. **journalofregressiontherapy.com**

If you're interested in what's happening in the arena of scientific investigation of past life memories, the Division of Perceptual Studies, a unit of the Department of Psychiatry and Neurobehavioral Sciences at the University of Virginia, in Charlottesville, is worth your attention. This research unit was founded at UVA by well-known past life researcher Dr. Ian Stevenson in 1967, and his work is now being carried on by Dr. Jim Tucker. Utilizing scientific methods, the researchers investigate children who appear to have past life memories. **https://med.virginia.edu/perceptual-studies/**

Regression work—especially the portion that deals with the spiritual experiences between lifetimes—overlaps with the topic of near-death experiences. The International Association for Near Death Studies (IANDS) puts on an annual conference with many wonderful speakers and is open to non-NDE survivors as well as NDE'ers. Check out the website for many fascinating and inspiring NDE stories and future events planned by IANDS. Membership in the association is quite reasonable and you can stay abreast of the latest research via their newsletter. **www.IANDS.org**

The Transpersonal Consultation Group maintains an extensive library of material channeled by my dear friend and teacher Dr. Ron Scolastico. This is a tremendous resource if you are looking for spiritual inspiration, meditation instruction, and an understanding of the big picture of our earth adventure. Ron's wife, Susan Scolastico, is carrying on Ron's work after his death. **www.ronscolastico.com**

I mentioned the use of tapping, or EFT (emotional freedom technique), in some client stories. This is a wonderful tool that you can apply for yourself to help work through a variety of issues. EFT was recently catapulted into popular attention by Nick Ortner, author of *The Tapping Solution: A Revolutionary System for Stress-Free Living*, but it has been around for a number of years. I particularly like the work of Lindsay Kenny, EFT master at Progressive EFT; she works with what she calls "reversals," those limiting, unconscious beliefs that are standing in the way of our achieving our goals. **www.proeft.com; www.thetappingsolution.com**

If you want to keep reading about past life therapy, there are a number of wonderful books on the suggested reading list on my website. Check my blog on the website for ongoing news. **www.pastlives.org**

Appendix B:

How Do We Access

Past Life Memories?

MOST OFTEN, past life memories are explored through the use of hypnotic regression, which means you are put into a "hypnotic" or highly relaxed state, and then "regressed" (moved backward) to an earlier time.

If you have never undergone hypnosis before, you may have a number of misunderstandings about what it is and how it works. Quite simply, it is a way of entering a level of relaxation whereby your memory is enhanced and the limits and constraints of the logical, conscious mind can be bypassed. In this state we gain access more easily to the unconscious mind, enabling us to call up images, symbols, and things we have forgotten consciously—just as we do when we're dreaming. In hypnosis, however, you are not "asleep." Other than being very relaxed, you remain aware and conscious of what is going on around you, even while being able to focus on inner images and feelings more completely. That's a good thing, because if my clients were not able to communicate with me throughout the session, I would not know what they were experiencing and how to guide them through it!

For those who meditate, hypnosis feels familiar to a meditative state. You do not "give up control" to the therapist; in fact, you give feedback and remain in control of the session at all times. And although the therapist can give you positive suggestions to help you in your normal conscious life (for example, when hypnosis is used to stop smoking or lose weight), no one can "program" you to do something that goes against your desires or beliefs. Those Las Vegas hypnotists who have people acting like chickens onstage are using volunteers who already have a major streak of exhibitionism in them, even if not consciously acknowledged.

When I conduct a past life session with a new client, I typically spend the first half hour talking with the individual to learn a little more about what it is they want to explore, what the history of the situation has been, and any ways in which they have tried to address it. I explain the process that we will be using in more detail and answer any questions the client may have. This also serves to establish some familiarity and ease before jumping into what can be rather intense work. In most cases, I guide clients through progressive muscle relaxation throughout their bodies, then use a variety of deepening techniques to move them to the optimal level of relaxation and inner focus to access their past life memories. This is called hypnotic induction. Then I use one of a variety of transitions to move them into a prior lifetime; for example, having their awareness float above their bodies and then return to earth in another time and place; walk down a hall with many doors and step through one particular door that beckons; or cross a special stream to another time and place— to name a few.

Some past life therapists choose not to use hypnosis to move clients into other lifetimes. In fact, Dr. Roger Woolger used to take great pride in the fact that he did not use the traditional hypnotic induction. Nonetheless, his clients would end up in a similar altered state; they just got there differently. I have found that I prefer to use hypnosis for a number of reasons. For one thing, I believe that most of us in this modern world could benefit from deeper levels of relax-ation and a quieting of our busy, conscious minds. So the hypnosis in itself is therapeutic. I also find that most clients believe that they need some special help to access these memories. By being led through a fifteen- to twenty-minute induction, they get beyond their disbelief that these memories may actually be close to the surface and easy to access. Above all else, I've found that using hypnosis works reliably for most clients, whereas the results with other techniques are a little more variable.

Appendix C:
Are You a Good Candidate
for Past Life Therapy?

SO HOW DO you know if you are a good candidate for a successful past life session? Here are some important considerations that impact the effectiveness of a regression:

1. Can you relax enough to do the work? If you find that you are always wound up, unable to relax, and can't ever quiet your mind, it will be difficult for you to reach the level of relaxation that is usually necessary to go deeply into past life memories. It doesn't mean it's impossible, but you may need to practice for a while before attempting to recall prior lifetimes. Try some yoga, meditation, qigong, or relaxation CDs.

2. Have you attempted to address the issue in a more conventional manner? Past life work is not a magic bullet to deal with whatever troubles you have, especially if you haven't given it some time and attention beforehand. Would you say you have some insight into your current

life and situation, that you've worked on yourself,
or perhaps sought other professional help?

3. Can you suspend your disbelief long enough to allow
a session to unfold? You don't have to firmly believe in
reincarnation for past life therapy to be very effective.
We can always treat the story as therapeutic imagery that
speaks to the pertinent issues in your current life and
garners excellent results. However, you need to be open
to the possibility that this approach will yield something
helpful.

4. Are you able to open up and be vulnerable when in a safe
and protected environment? The interaction between
client and therapist can be intense as we walk through past
life memories together and see the emotional impact they
have had. The client never gives up control but does need
to be able to trust the therapist as a guide in the process.

Appendix D:

Integrating a Past

Life Session

I ALWAYS PROVIDE a summary sheet at the end of a client session that captures the most salient points and helps the client to integrate the experience into their current life. My summary sheet covers the following topics:

- *Key Lessons from the Lifetime.* What were the lessons learned from that life experience? Were there lessons that were unintended and possibly not helpful but learned nonetheless (for example, "You can't trust people.")? Were there potential lessons that were missed? What else could have been learned from this life experience?

- *Pertinence to the Current Life.* Why was it important for the client to see this lifetime today? In what ways does it relate to his/her current life? Is the client still working on the same themes and lessons or has he/she mastered them? Where does he/she see contrasts and/or similarities between then and now?

- *Spiritual Guidance.* I list the key messages from the client's higher guidance. This is often the richest part of the regression summary.

- *Recommended Steps.* This is where I include my suggestions as a therapist that I believe would help the client continue to integrate the work we've done and move forward in their current life. It may include writing assignments, meditation exercises, or a variety of therapeutic "homework assignments."

Notes

Chapter 1: Out of the New Age and into the Mainstream

1. Frank Newport and Maura Strausberg, "Americans' Belief in Psychic and Paranormal Phenomena Is Up over Last Decade," Gallup Poll, June 8, 2001, http://www.gallup.com/poll/4483/americans-belief-psychic-para normal-phenomena-over-last-decade.aspx.
2. "Americans' Belief in God, Miracles and Heaven Declines," The Harris Poll, December 16, 2013, http://www.theharrispoll.com/health-and-life /Americans__Belief_in_God__Miracles_and_Heaven_Declines.html.
3. Lisa Miller, "Remembrances of Lives Past," *New York Times*, August 27, 2010, http://www.nytimes.com/2010/08/29/fashion/29PastLives.html?_r=0.

ABOUT THE AUTHOR

After earning her master's degree in counseling psychology at Santa Clara University, Ann Barham pursued a traditional counseling practice for a number of years. In time, the understanding that there was something additional calling her led her to pursue past life therapy. She found it to be another means of helping people rapidly, effectively, and on more levels simultaneously—emotionally, physically, and spiritually—than conventional counseling approaches alone allowed. After training with some of the world's best-known experts on past life work at that time, including Dr. Brian Weiss and the late Dr. Roger Woolger, Barham gradually began to focus her professional attention almost exclusively on past life therapy.

Barham holds a license as a marriage and family therapist in the state of California, and certification as a past life therapist with the International Board for Regression Therapy. She lives and bases her work in the town of Gilroy, California, world famous for its garlic festival every summer.

You can visit Barham's website at www.pastlives.org; follow her on Twitter: @PastLifetimes; or connect with her on Facebook: www.Facebook.com/ExploringPastLives.

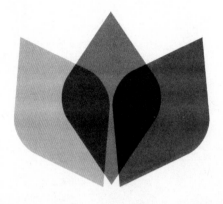

ENLIVEN™

About Our Books: We are the world's first holistic publisher for mission-driven authors. We curate, create, collaborate on, and commission sophisticated, fresh titles and voices to enhance your spiritual development, success, and wellness pursuits.

About Our Vision: Our authors are the voice of empowerment, creativity, and spirituality in the twenty-first century. You, our readers, are brilliant seekers of adventure, unexpected stories, and tools to transform yourselves and your world. Together, we are change-makers on a mission to increase literacy, uplift humanity, ignite genius, and create reasons to gather around books. We think of ourselves as instigators of soulful exchange.

Welcome to the wondrous world of Enliven Books, a new imprint from Zhena Muzyka, author of *Life by the Cup: Inspiration for a Purpose-Filled Life*, and Atria, an imprint of Simon & Schuster, Inc.

To explore our list of books and learn about fresh new voices in the realm of Mind-Body-Spirit, please visit us at

EnlivenBooks.com | **/EnlivenBooks**